*Hand Woolcombing
and Spinning*

Hand Woolcombing and Spinning

A Guide to Worsteds from the Spinning-Wheel

Peter Teal

BLANDFORD PRESS
POOLE · NEW YORK · SYDNEY

First published in the UK 1976 by Blandford Press
Link House, West Street, Poole, Dorset BH15 1LL
Reprinted 1979

First published in this paperback edition 1985
Reprinted 1986

Distributed in the United States by
Sterling Publishing Co, Inc,
2 Park Avenue, New York, NY 10016

Distributed in Australia by
Capricorn Link (Australia) Pty Ltd
PO Box 665, Lane Cove, NSW 2066

ISBN 0 7137 1645 2

Printed in Great Britain by Robert Hartnoll (1985) Ltd., Bodmin, Cornwall.

Contents

To the Memory of my Father,
Harold Teal,
the Wiltshire Bee-Master,
I affectionately dedicate
this book

Acknowledgements

It is easy enough to sit down and write a book about your work, but you very quickly find that your knowledge is not self-engendered. Much of it is your interpretation of things other people have written or said. Whenever I have become aware that my material is not original, I have traced the source and asked permission to use it. Everyone so approached has willingly given their blessing to my work. If I have inadvertently omitted any source, I apologize most humbly.

It is often obligatory to say 'without the help of my dear wife this work would not have been possible'. How does one state a plain truth without making it sound trite? She took my roughly-typed script and re-typed it; she advised on grammar and content. Her kitchen was transformed into a wool-comber's shop for weeks on end. Her sitting-room was cluttered with spinning-wheels. She was model, lighting boy and shutter-puncher. So, what more can I say than 'without the help of my dear wife, this work would not have been possible'.

My thanks go to the Metropolitan Borough of Calderdale, who allowed me to draw freely upon their booklet *Hand Wool Combing*, by H. L. Roth, and their publication *From Fleece to Yarn*; to the Textile Institute for permission to use the drawing of the Big Wheel in use and the wool-comber's pad; to the British Wool Marketing Board for all their help and permission to use their Definition of Terms; to Langham Photographic Instruments, who supplied the 320 watt-sec. electronic flash unit with which the photographs were taken; to the Wool Industries Research Association for all the information and help they have given me over the years, without which this book would have been considerably impoverished; and to the British Museum for permission to reproduce the 'Martyrdom of Bishop Blaize'.

Introduction

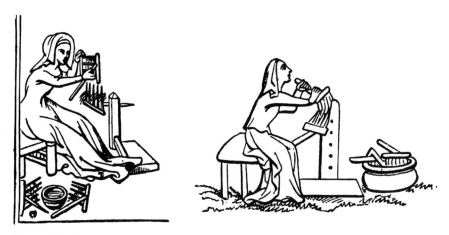

Woman hand woolcombing in the Middle Ages. From a manuscript in the British Museum, believed to date from the end of the 13th or the beginning of the 14th century.

I make no apology for claiming that worsted yarns are the élite among all those which can be spun from wool fibres. They are smooth, lustrous yarns, often exhibiting a sheen akin to that of a pearl.

Because worsted spinners use wools of longer staple than those used by woollen spinners, a knowledge of worsted spinning will greatly increase the range of yarns a hand-spinner can produce. It will enable variety to be added to woven structures by using worsted warps with woollen weft and, by using the long staple for the warp and the short for the weft, to make better use of the range of fibres a fleece contains.

The spinner/weaver can make use of the lustre by employing yarns twisted clockwise ('Z') or anti-clockwise ('S') in the warp; this will impart a distinctive and subtle light-reflecting quality, or colour variation when dyed yarns are used. Knitters will find that patterns relying upon colour will be more clearly defined, and that their garments will have a sheen entirely lacking in woollen spun yarns. Yarns composed of fibres of different colours blended together become an accurately-repeatable economic process in terms of time, one ounce of roving of a three-colour blend an hour becoming an easily sustained norm.

Because there are no whiskers or lumps or slubs to mar their contours, any imperfections are glaringly obvious. A worsted spinner must therefore be a perfectionist; *there can be no second-best . . . ever.*

Such perfection can only be achieved by the spinner's having a complete understanding of the whole process, an understanding of the fibre selection and preparation, of yarn qualities, of the twisting process (spinning), and of the tools to be used.

But, first, what are the essential differences that set worsted yarns apart from others spun from wool fibres?

There are four altogether. Firstly, worsteds are made from the longer wool fibres, anything from 4 to 10 inches (10 to 25 cm) in staple length. The short fibres are removed by the combing process. Woollens are made from short fibres only.

Secondly, worsted yarns are spun (twisted) from rovings in which the fibres are truly parallel, the rovings being made from combed sliver. Woollens are spun from rolags of carded fibre, characterized by a more or less random fibre lay.

Thirdly, a roving is spun without any twist entering the drafting zone— that is the area where the roving is attenuated to spinning density. Rolags are spun by allowing the twist to enter and influence constituent fibres, which are extracted after they have been caught up by the twist.

Finally (a little outside the scope of this book), when worsted yarns are woven or knitted, no attempt is made to destroy their clarity of line, their smoothness, their lustre. Woollens, on the other hand, are subject to a finishing process the aim of which is to felt the fibres into a smooth, dense fabric.

Although I have seen hand-spinners at work in all parts of the United Kingdom, in their homes, at exhibitions, at Guild meetings, I have never seen a single person preparing fibre for, and spinning, a true worsted yarn. From my friends all over the world I find this also to be the pattern in other countries.

This is hardly surprising when you come face to face with the tools required; the combs are enough to put anyone off and to turn her mind towards the much gentler-looking carders. Wool combs are not only unpleasant to contemplate, but they can be heavy and cumbersome to use, and since hand-spinning has tended to be largely a female occupation, it was probably felt by the people who re-vitalized the process in the mid-1800s that such tools were beyond the powers of the (then) 'weaker sex'. Two world wars later, we recognize that women are as capable of sustained physical effort as men. There is nothing in the wool-combing process which is beyond the strength of a healthy female; those who are somewhat advanced in years can use combs which are smaller in size than the 'standard'.

I have been spinning worsted yarns for eight years, and it is the experience gained over that period which I have detailed in this book. My work has followed closely the accepted methods, as told by the few practising wool combers who recorded their skills. Some of the information I have gained empirically or by a process of reason; some came as flashes of inspiration. I do not pretend to know the whole story; I am still learning, continually developing new ideas and skills. You too will develop along lines personal to you, leading perhaps by different paths towards the same end.

The purpose of this book is primarily to encourage you to investigate and adopt worsted spinning; by showing you first how to produce the necessary tools, and then a yarn, the quality of which, with practice, may rival that of the industrially produced machine-spun thread, and so lift your spinning out of the rut in which common or garden woollen-spun yarns have lain for the past century.

To understand how the present methods of hand-spinning evolved I think we must revert to the days when the trade was flourishing, some time prior to 1770, when the spinning-jennies were already ousting the spinning-wheel.

For decades every cottage in the British textile-producing areas had its spinning-wheel, at which the spinster would work, either sitting or standing—for these were Big Wheels, not the Saxony Wheels in common use today.

It is not known how a weaver gave details of his yarn requirements to the spinner, or how the spinner was trained to comply with them, but we can surmise that, since it took from four to six spinners to produce enough yarn for one weaver, there must have been some close similarity in yarns from one spinner to another, or his task would have been impossible. But these spinsters were cottagers, illiterate; it was, after all, a very lowly order of work, so that, when the jennies came along and the spinsters found their wheels idle for ever-lengthening periods, they turned to other means of making a livelihood, if they could.

In one generation, hand-spinning died as a trade. In another generation, most of those actively engaged in the trade had also died, and since no-one able to write about the trade ever did so, they took their knowledge with them to the grave.

By the time people again became interested in hand-spinning, they had largely to start from scratch, and it has to be said that they did not make a very good job of it.

It is perhaps unfortunate that the new corps of hand-spinners, being educated people and quite definitely not 'working-class', elevated hand-spinning from a trade to a craft, away from the people with the practical heritage who might have helped. It has remained ever since as something clever to do, something different to talk about, practised by people who have been so lacking in perception that few have ever bothered to understand their machines or to relate their product to the commercially available yarns they affect to scorn, but which they can never emulate.

Every would-be spinner should suspend from her distaff a length of machine-spun thread, the perfection of which should be the goal at which to aim.

So often the cry is, 'But it is the very perfection, the very uniformity of machine-spun thread from which we strive to get away'; but is it? Is it not more truthful to say that the yarns produced, instantly recognizable as 'home spun', are that way because the spinners cannot do any better?

'But we want yarns of character', they cry! Of course we do, all of us, but let it be a good character we give them. Let us first produce a plain yarn perfectly, and then doctor it in some way to produce the 'character', if you must. But you know, I am almost willing to have a bet with you that, by the time you can produce a really perfect plain spun yarn, you will be so proud of it for the beautiful thing it is, you will be extremely loth to adulterate it in any way!

Of course this does pose the question: 'If we are going to make hand-spun yarns as perfectly as machine-spun products, why bother; why not just buy the yarns of commerce and have done with it?'

The short answer to that is that economic pressures on the spinning industry prevents their making exactly the yarns we require. There are yarns we can use, yes, provided we limit or adapt our construction to suit those which are available. But the hand-spinner who thoroughly understands the trade has complete freedom to design a material conforming to the very highest standards. One can determine the diameter of yarns, the amount of twist they contain, their colour, and the manner in which they are used. The resulting products will therefore be of unsurpassable quality and completely exclusive, but one thing they will not be is instantly identifiable as 'home spun'.

We at least will hang up our piece of machine-spun yarn, and when we can produce a similar length, as uniform in diameter, in fibre content and in twist content, we can call ourselves spinners, and be justifiably proud of our product.

How long will it take? You should, if you practise for six hours a day, produce a fairly reasonable yarn in three days. This, at any rate, is the time I allow my students. It may take a further month of concentrated work for the process to become an effortlessly automatic un-thought-about movement of hand and foot. You should then be able to produce a yarn of a particular type with the minimum of effort and the maximum of pleasure.

You will probably find it awkward at first, after this initial training, to change your fingering and treadling to suit yarns of different types, but the more practice you have the easier the job will become. Of course, it may sometimes happen that, even after prolonged practice, the desired synchronization just will not come. That is the time to leave it—to go out for a walk, forget it, and not to try again until you are completely relaxed and fresh.

Remember, practice *does* make perfect. There are *no* short cuts. We are embarking upon a period of concentrated work . . . so, if you will hang up your length of machine-spun thread, we will begin.

Chapter 1

The Tools

Wool Combs, Pad, Diz, Oiler and Water Spray

An essential requirement for successful worsted spinning is that the fibres should be absolutely parallel when they are twisted, but the various processes through which they have gone before reaching the spinner, shearing, sorting, scouring, dyeing, drying, etc. all tend to tangle the fibres and disarrange their natural orderliness. It is therefore essential that they should be treated in some way prior to spinning to restore them once again to a near-parallel state.

The tools used for this job were the wool combs—the cause, you might say, of all the bother. For there is no doubt that they were cumbersome implements, made as large as a man could conveniently wield all day, and weighing between five and eight pounds (about 2 to $3\frac{1}{2}$ kg) each.

We are told that wool combers were tough, independent men, that they carefully controlled the numbers employed in the trade—only the eldest son of a wool comber, for instance, could become apprenticed to it—that they had a trade association and held meetings at a time when it was illegal to do so, and that because of their monopolistic control of the trade, they were able to obtain for themselves a higher than average wage, or rate for the job. They were the aristocrats, in the sense of being the most well paid, of the textile workers.

Unlike that of the hand-spinners, whose trade was killed by the jennies and mules, the work of the wool combers was exceedingly difficult to mechanize, and so they were the last of the hand workers to fall to the machine. When, in 1850, Lister perfected his mechanical combing device, it only took a decade to see the complete eradication of this once powerful and numerous body of tradesmen.

Writers are unanimous in asserting that wool combing was an arduous occupation. The huge combs were heated on stoves, the fumes from which often made working conditions unpleasant. The heat from the stoves, combined with their heavy labours, made the workers sweat . . . beer-drinking was the method often employed to replace the evaporated moisture, and the intemperance of the trade was a by-word.

14

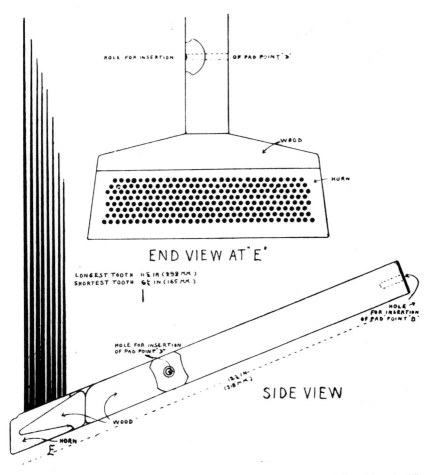

HOLE FOR INSERTION OF PAD POINT 'D'

WOOD

HORN

END VIEW AT 'E'

LONGEST TOOTH 11⅝ IN (298 MM)
SHORTEST TOOTH 6½ IN (165 MM)

HOLE FOR INSERTION OF PAD POINT 'D'

HOLE FOR INSERTION OF PAD POINT 'D'

12½ IN (318 MM)

SIDE VIEW

WOOD

HORN

E

Fig. 1   The eight-pitch comb for very fine wool from Hand Wool Combing *by H. Ling Roth. Length overall 12½ in (318 mm).*

I hasten to add that wool combing, in the way we shall do it, does not lead to any similar bad habits or odours!

It must be admitted that wool combs are dangerous-looking implements, which probably explains why, after the re-introduction of hand-spinning, the ladies who were largely responsible looked more towards cards as the tools most suitable for use around the home.

Even in museums, wool combs are fairly rare exhibits. Those I use, and

15

shall describe, are modified from a drawing which appears in a book called *Hand Wool Combing* by H. Ling Roth, and which is again available as a reprint combined with *Methods of Hand Spinning in Egypt and the Sudan*, from the Museums Service of the Metropolitan Borough of Calderdale, Halifax, England (Fig. 1).

The combs made as illustrated weighed about eight pounds (about $3\frac{1}{2}$ kg) each, and were quite beyond my ability to use for any sustained period. The number of rows of tines (or teeth or broitches) calibrated the combs. Three rows = a 3-pitch comb, four rows = a 4-pitch comb, and so on, up to a maximum of 8. We are told that a 3-pitch comb might be used for a coarse fleece, a 5-pitch for a Lincoln, and an 8-pitch for a South Down or Merino.

Eventually I reduced the rows of tines from 8 to 4 and the number of tines in a row from 32 to 19 . . . which just about halved the weight. (See Fig. 2, with dimensions in the table.)

In making even smaller and lighter combs, I advocate a reduction in the width rather than in the number of rows of tines. Experience has shown that the deeper the area for holding the fibre, the more chance there is for the short hairs and fibres (noils), double cuts (where the shearer has had two cuts at a lock, leaving a lump of short stubbly fibres of anything up to an inch long) and dross to be held back from the sliver, resulting in a considerable improvement in yarn quality. I have found that 4 rows (a 4-pitch comb) is a happy compromise of weight and efficiency.

Each wool comb consists of a head, back, set of tines and a handle. The timber I chose for the head was teak, because I thought it would be less liable to shrink and loosen the tines when the combs were heated. Teak has good dimensional stability and seems to stand up to the job very well. Iroko would probably serve just as well and oak may possibly be even better, in that the tannin it contains would help to fix the tines by rusting them in place. However, since I found that teak did the job perfectly, I thought the extra expense justified, and have used it ever since.

The tines have to be set at an angle of 70 degrees. This is easily accomplished if the edge of the plank from which the heads are to be made is planed to the correct angle before the head section is parted off (Fig. 3).

Each section can then be marked out for drilling. Great accuracy is required and care must be taken to ensure that the centre-to-centre distances are accurate in every case. If many combs are to be made, it will save time if a metal template corresponding exactly in size to the head of

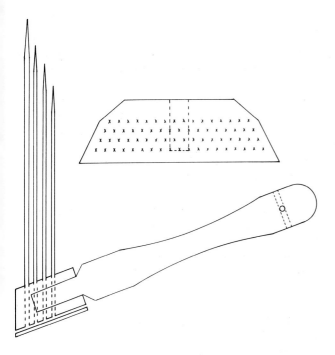

Fig. 2   Drawing for standard 40-g load four-pitch comb.

Dimensions for Standard 4-pitch Combs
of 20, 30 and 40g Working Load

Working Load	Comb Head	Handle	Tines				Weight
			Row 1	Row 2	Row 3	Row 4	
40 g	mm 205×75×40	305×40	19:305×5	18:280×3·2	17:250×3.2	16:230×3.2	1984 g
1·5 oz	in 8×3×1½	12×1½	19:12×$\frac{3}{16}$	18:11×$\frac{1}{8}$	17:10×$\frac{1}{8}$	16:9×$\frac{1}{8}$	70 oz
30 g	mm 150×75×40	280×40	15:250×5	14:230×3·2	13:205×3·2	12:180×2·3	1360 g
1 oz	in 6×3×1½	11×1½	15:10×$\frac{3}{16}$	14:9×$\frac{1}{8}$	13:8×$\frac{1}{8}$	12:7$\frac{3}{32}$	48 oz
20 g	mm 115×70×40	230×40	11:205×3·2	10:185×3·2	9:165×3·2	8:145×2·3	652 g
$\frac{3}{4}$ oz	in 4½×2¾×1½	9×1½	11:8×$\frac{1}{8}$	10:7¼×$\frac{1}{8}$	9:6½×$\frac{1}{8}$	8:5¾×$\frac{3}{32}$	23 oz

17

Fig. 3   *Workpiece for two comb heads, angle planed and marked out for drilling handle holes and parting off. Holes would have been drilled before the angled face was planed if a pillar drill was used.*

Fig. 4   *Drilling the tine holes on a lathe fitted with a compound table.*

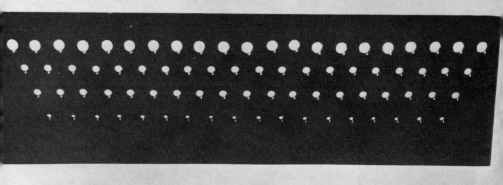

Fig. 5   *Metal template in which holes have been drilled at a 70° angle to support the drill tip. Make the template for the largest comb head and it can be used for any comb size.*

Fig. 6   *Metal template screwed to comb head for direct drilling without prior marking out.*

the comb is made and drilled the exact size of a small centre punch. It can then be clamped or screwed to the comb head and will ensure that each successive head is marked in an identical manner without the tedious necessity of dividing out each hole individually. If the head is to be drilled without the aid of a template, then in any case each point to be drilled must be centre-punched to ensure that the drill does not wander off centre. Remember that the drill will enter the work at a 70-degree angle to the face.

The first time I did the job I scaled up the drawing in Ling Roth's book and drilled all the holes as indicated. But when I attempted to force in the tines the timber parted along what was little more than a perforation! On the second attempt I increased the centre-to-centre distance to $\frac{3}{8}$ inch (9·5 mm) and that effectively prevented any recurrence of the problem.

I have no idea how the wool combers of old worked, but I think they must have had a jig of some sort to enable them to drill so many holes with the degree of accuracy that is required.

If you have a lathe with a compound table, then the job is fairly easy. The head is mounted on the previously planed and angled surface and fed to the drill, the table being dropped $\frac{3}{8}$ inch after each row of holes (Fig. 4).

Again, much time and trouble can be saved if a stout metal template has been fixed to the face of the work. This one will be a little more difficult to make, though, because the holes will have to be drilled to the prescribed 70 degrees, a matter which may be a little more difficult in metal. It is a job that would pay dividends because the metal, say $\frac{1}{8}$ inch (3 mm) thick, would support the head of the drill as it entered the work and prevent any tendency it may have to wander (Figs 5 and 6).

I think this is an occasion when I would advocate engineer's twist drills, and short ones at that, for the work. They will make a much cleaner and more accurate hole than their counterparts for woodwork. Since I find that to ensure a really tight fit of the tine in the hole, it should be drilled $\frac{1}{64}$ inch (0·4 mm) undersize of the tine, you may well find that such a drill size is unobtainable in anything but an engineer's drill anyway. Use a slow speed and feed, and the drill will not heat up. Drill right through the comb head.

A very simple jig can be constructed to enable you to do the job speedily on an ordinary vertical or pillar drill (see Figs 7 and 8). The jig has a table which slopes at 70 degrees, with a ledge along the lower edge against which the angled face of the comb bears. Between this ledge and the comb head to be drilled are placed 3 laths, each $\frac{3}{8}$ inch (9·5 mm) thick. The jig is fixed to the drill table with the work piece and 3 laths in position, so that the

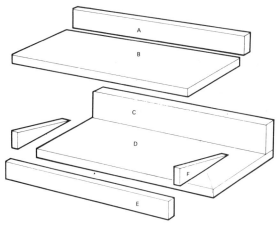

Fig. 7(a)   A Laths,   3 off $16 \times 1\frac{1}{2} \times \frac{3}{8}$ in ($410 \times 40 \times 9$ mm)
            B Platform,   1 off $16 \times 5\frac{1}{4} \times \frac{1}{2}$ in ($410 \times 134 \times 12$ mm)
            C Front,   1 off $16 \times 2\frac{1}{2} \times \frac{3}{4}$ in ($410 \times 63 \times 19$ mm)
            D Base,   1 off $16 \times 5\frac{3}{4} \times \frac{1}{2}$ in ($410 \times 146 \times 12$ mm)
            E Back,   1 off $15 \times 1\frac{7}{8} \times \frac{3}{4}$ in ($380 \times 48 \times 19$ mm)
            F Platform

               Supports,   2 off $5 \times 1\frac{7}{8} \times \frac{1}{2}$ in ($127 \times 48 \times 12$ mm)
               Supports (*F*) *can be cut from one piece* $5 \times 1\frac{7}{8} \times \frac{1}{2}$ *in, by sawing across the diagonal if an allowance is made for the thickness of the sawcut.*
               B must be planed to 70° where it butts against C, and along the rear edge to bring it parallel with E.
               E must be planed to 70° along its top edge so that it will drop in flush between F, F, D and B.

Fig. 7   *Drilling jig made from deal. It should be large enough to accommodate the largest comb head. Make three laths for a four-pitch comb.*

Fig. 8 Comb head and drilling template mounted on drilling jig.

Fig. 9 Using the drilling jig on a vertical pillar drill.

work can be slid from left to right with the line of centre pops—or holes in the template if you are using one—exactly under the drill tip (Fig. 9).

The row of holes nearest to the laths is drilled first, of course, after which one lath is removed and another row of holes drilled, followed by the removal of another lath after that row of holes . . . and so on.

Fit the comb handle before the holes are drilled so that the tines can pass right through it and lock it in position.

When you have the metal you propose to use for the tines, carry out some tests to find what drill size is required to secure a tine firmly; $\frac{1}{64}$ inch under the metal size usually provides a pretty tight fit.

When the blanks for the comb head have been roughed out and the hole for the handle drilled, lay them on one side while the two handles are m Leave all dimensions about $\frac{1}{32}$ inch (0·8 mm) oversize, and put l handles and comb heads in a dry warm space for a few days—a week e if you have that sort of patience. An airing cupboard is ideal.

If you do that, and finally turn the handles to a dead tight fit for the hole in the comb head, the two will stay tightly joined for life. Failure to take this action can often result in handles that work loose after only a few months of use. The root cause is the near impossibility of finding seasoned timber these days. If you turn up a handle from timber straight from the yard it will have a high moisture content; as it dries out the timber will shrink and the joint will become sloppy.

If you can pre-shrink (season) the timber and then turn it to size it should never work loose. Seasoning is not a job you can rush. People fail to realize that as the outer layer of cells dry out they tend to form an insulating coat for those underneath. If you try to rush the process by using too high a temperature you can irreversibly damage the material by causing cracks (shakes) through the artificial imbalance created between the dry external cells and the still moist insulated internal cells.

Make the handle a comfortable shape to hold, narrower where it is gripped, where it fits the palm of the hand (Fig. 10). It is essential that each handle should be identical. Study the drawing of the pad and you will see that the handle must slide snugly into it.

Fig. 10   Comb head and handles ready for assembly and drilling.

Fig. 11   For pointing the tines—a
¼-in (6 mm) electric drill and a
power grindstone.

Fig. 12   Tine rods wired in bundles
and held between V blocks for
sawing off.

I must confess that finding tine material was a headache. At first I tried
to find some pointed rod that could be adapted, but after much fruitless
searching I finally had to find the metal and make them myself. Eventually
I tried oxy-acetylene welding rod. This worked perfectly, had good springy
qualities, and even had a copper coating to protect it from rust. But before
you go dashing off to buy any, I should warn you that the copper coating
was a real curse! The oil and water used in the combing caused a skin of
verdigris to form on the tines which, before I had discovered the source,
had stained several combings a pale green.

You will find that welding rod can be obtained uncoated, and this is the
material to use.

For the standard full-size combs, you will require nineteen 12-inch long
by $\frac{3}{16}$-inch diameter (30·5 cm × 5 mm) tines, eighteen 11-inch long by
$\frac{1}{8}$-inch diameter (28 cm × 3·2 mm) tines, seventeen 10-inch long by $\frac{1}{8}$-inch
diameter (25·4 cm × 3·2 mm) tines, and sixteen 9-inch long by $\frac{1}{8}$-inch diameter (23 cm × 3·2 mm) tines for each comb.

I found pointing the tines a dreary business. With 140 rods to point, you
just have to slog on. My method requires an electric drill and a power
grindstone, either a bench model or one that fits on the lathe (Fig. 11).

Work out how many tines you will be able to cut from one length of rod,
and wire the requisite number of rods together. Cut two V-blocks from
hard wood (beech will do) and with one V-block on each vice jaw, grip the
bundle of rods near the point at which they are to be cut. This will save an
enormous amount of time over cutting them off individually. Cut all the
$\frac{3}{16}$-inch (5 mm) tines first, for you may find it necessary to plane a little off
the V's when it comes to gripping the smaller diameter bundles. If you
wire the bundles about half-way between the points to be cut, you should
not have much trouble (Fig. 12).

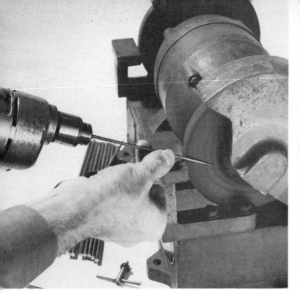

Fig. 13 Hold the tine on the right-hand side of the grindstone where the surface opposes the tine rotation.

Fig. 14 Smoothness is a relative quality, as you can see from a close-up of tines direct from a 'smooth' stone.

The rods are secured in turn in the electric drill chuck, and the drill started. Some rods run true, others tend to waggle about a bit, but they all steady up when they come in contact with the grindstone. The grindstone will be rotating in a vertical plane, towards you. As you look at it, the surface you see will be falling downwards. The tine in the drill will be rotating in a clockwise direction when viewed from the accelerator end, so if the tine is held against the left-hand side of the grindstone the two surfaces will be travelling in the same direction. More efficiency will result if the two surfaces are moving in opposite directions, so move the tine to the right-hand side of the stone and all should be well. I use the side of the stone because there is usually a larger working surface there than across the face. (See Fig. 13.)

The point angle is not critical, but should be as long as possible; about 1½ inches (37 mm) of taper is ideal on the larger tines, reduced to perhaps 1 inch (25 mm) on the smaller. Do not rush the job; try not to heat the tine to incandescence. Dip it in water when it starts to go blue.

If you have a double-ended grindstone, then, after removing most of the metal on the coarse stone (with, no doubt, a gratifying shower of sparks), you can smooth the tine down on the fine stone (Fig. 14).

The point should be really smooth and shiny. To finish off the tine, I found it best to prepare a board with some emery cloth tacked on to it. I discovered that if the tine was pressed quite hard on to the cloth a bright finish appeared in no time. Move the point about a bit; do not keep it running in one place or you will soon wear a hole in the emery cloth (Fig. 15).

You should be able to do the whole operation on one tine without removing it from the drill, or even stopping the drill. Each tine need only be handled once, and by the time you reach the last one you should have a good work flow going.

Fixing the tines into the comb head must be done with care, for they are driven in, point end first, from the top of the comb. It is absolutely essential that the comb head should be well supported near the point where the tine is being driven home, for there is considerable danger that the head, perforated along the lines of the tine holes, will snap.

I find the job can be done easily if the comb head rests on the edge of the bench, the handle supported by one hand. The row of tines nearest the handle are fitted first. Always fit one tine at each end of the row first, then the comb head can be pushed up against the edge of the bench, ensuring the maximum support for the comb head, but at the same time preventing a tine being accidentally driven into the bench, thus effectively spiking the head and bench together! (Fig. 16).

Fig. 15 I add ordinary lubricating oil and a little powdered carborundum lapping compound to the emery to produce a really fine finish. (Motor car engine valve grinding compound would also be satisfactory).

Fig. 16 Support the head close to the point where the tine is driven home. Use the edge of the bench or a block of wood.

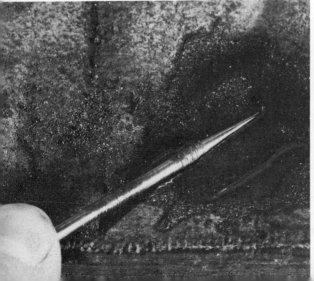

Fig. 17 The cap gives the comb a professional finish.

Fig. 18 'The Family'—20, 30 and 40-g wool combs.

Drive them home flush with the top surface of the comb head and, when all are in place, the cap can be fitted—admittedly a cap is not essential, but the combs look so much more professional with them, and the additional effort required is slight. It can be the same timber as the head, or one contrasting in colour (Fig. 17). Invert the head upon it and mark all around the contour. Cut the cap dead to size and secure in place with four countersunk screws. You may prefer to cut the cap slightly oversize and then sand it down to an exact fit after it has been screwed in place. Round off all the exposed edges and your combs will have a thoroughly professional appearance (Figs 18 and 19).

Fig. 19 When not in use, make the combs 'safe' by sliding the pointed ends in towards each head.

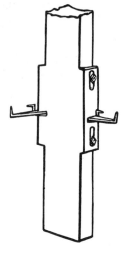

Fig. 20   Traditional   woolcomber's pad, fixed to a stout pole which rose from floor to ceiling.

When in use the combs were fixed on a 'pad' or holder which was often attached to a post rising from floor to ceiling. The 'pad' was a metal device which held the comb firmly with the tines either vertical or horizontal (Fig. 20).

The pads I use are far simpler and can be secured to any flat surface at a convenient working height. I think they are better, too, because the thrust of combing is taken right where it is exerted, on the head, not half-way down the handle, as it is on traditional pads.

As we shall see, at one stage of the operation the combs must be vertical and at another horizontal. The pad must be so constructed that it will hold the comb securely in both positions.

My pad is made from 1-inch (25 mm) timber, and consists of a base, upon which are secured two battens to hold the comb straight, a top plate to secure the comb and a removeable peg to prevent the comb from pulling out in use (Fig. 21).

In the centre of the top is drilled a $\frac{3}{16}$-inch (5 mm) hole to take the peg which will locate the comb. The pad illustrated is drilled to take three sizes of combs.

The base plate of the pad is cut away on one side in the front to allow the comb to tilt into a horizontal position. That illustrated is for a left-handed person; that for the right-handed comber should have the front cut on the other side of the centre line, of course (Figs 22 and 23—dimensioned drawing).

Fig. 21 Woolcomber's pad made from high quality hard wood. Each comb is placed in position, pushed in as far as it will go, and a $\frac{3}{16}$-in (5-mm) drill passed down through the peg hole, once with the tines horizontal and once with them vertical.

Fig. 22 Component parts of the pad.

Fig. 23 Drawing and dimensions of the pad.

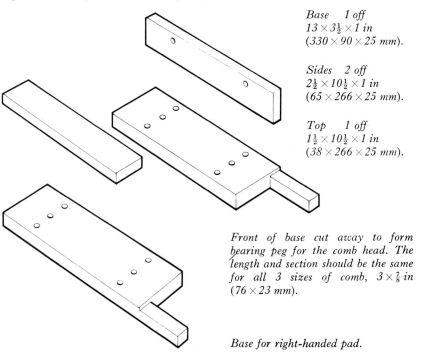

Base 1 off
$13 \times 3\frac{1}{2} \times 1$ in
($330 \times 90 \times 25$ mm).

Sides 2 off
$2\frac{1}{2} \times 10\frac{1}{2} \times 1$ in
($65 \times 266 \times 25$ mm).

Top 1 off
$1\frac{1}{2} \times 10\frac{1}{2} \times 1$ in
($38 \times 266 \times 25$ mm).

Front of base cut away to form bearing peg for the comb head. The length and section should be the same for all 3 sizes of comb, $3 \times \frac{7}{8}$ in (76×23 mm).

Base for right-handed pad.

29

Another tool you will require is the diz, a word some believe to be a local version of 'disc'. (See Fig. 24.)

The originals were made of horn, cow horn mostly, which is not easy to purchase these days. My local vet produced a couple for me . . . I had never examined one before, but the horn is an outer covering for a bone core, to which it is fixed by membranes. 'Don't know how you'll get the bone out,' he said, 'have fun', and departed.

I found one book which said 'bury the horn for two months', and another which told me to put it in a stream for a few weeks . . . so I buried one and put the other in the mill pond.

Since I wanted to start combing and couldn't bear the idea of having to wait possibly weeks for my diz, I purchased some plastic sheet and made one from that. I have to admit that it worked very well, even though I left it flat instead of curving it to cowhorn shape.

I left the horn in the earth alone, but occasionally I pulled the one out of the pond and tapped it against a stone, but it was six weeks before the bone core fell out . . . and then what a stench it made! A smell which, I'm glad to say, a few rinses in the stream removed. So I dug the one up from the garden and that core slipped out too . . . the stench was just as bad.

It was late summer when I got the horns; perhaps the bone retaining matter would have decomposed more quickly in really warm weather, or perhaps the cores can be boiled out. I just don't know.

I made my diz to the pattern shown in the Bankfield booklet, to get the curve right it meant cutting the horn off fairly high up, where it was very nearly solid (Fig. 25).

The section was slit down the middle, whereupon it was found to be much too thick and consequently too heavy. The walls should not be more than $\frac{1}{16}$ inch (1·5 mm) thick at the most.

I imagined the quickest way to remove the surplus material was to wear it away with the belt sander; it worked perfectly, and in no time at all the diz was down to the required thickness.

The horn gave off a distinctly blacksmith's shop, burnt hair smell when worked under pressure . . . what I did not realize was that all the fine particles being sanded off and being blown into my clothing also gave off the same smell! When I went indoors I was made to go smartly outside again to brush off all the dust. But it was no good. The horn particles had penetrated the weave, and it took a washing before all the smell was removed. So, be warned; if you sand the horn, either wear effective protective clothing, or stand well clear. You can, of course, file the horn away.

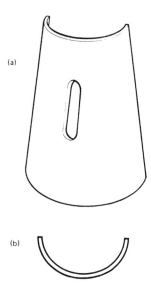

(a)

Fig. 24 The diz:

  (a) dimensions, 2 in (50 mm) high,
     slot $\frac{3}{16} \times \frac{1}{2}$ in (5 × 12 mm);

  (b) tracing made around base of diz.

(b)

Fig. 25 Cowhorn and diz which was made from the section that has been removed.

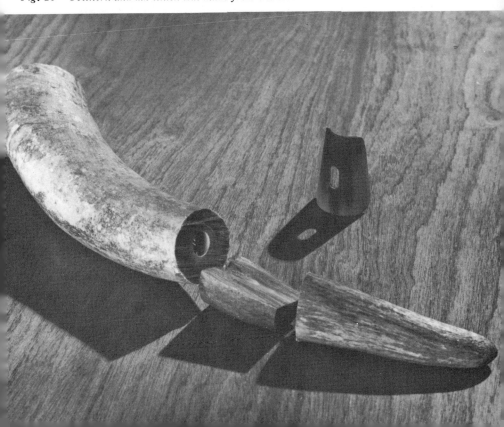

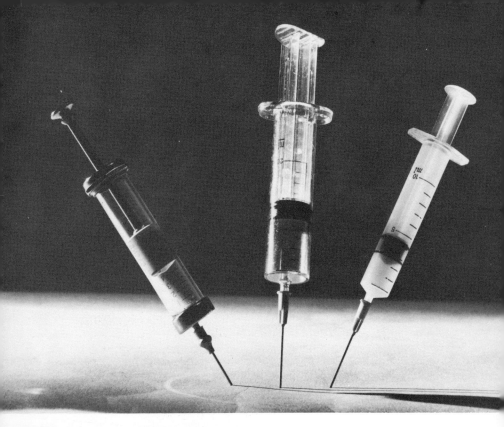

Fig. 26 On the left a 10-ml syringe with a ceramic piston and replaceable parts. Centre *and* right, *disposable syringes with rubber pistons.*

Fig. 27 Water spray, from cosmetic dispenser, delivers 1 ml of liquid per squirt.

Any scratches left on the diz can be removed first by successively finer grades of sandpaper, and later by metal polish. Tack a piece of old blanket on to a board, and drop pools of metal polish on that. The board will provide something firm against which to press and in no time at all you will have a surface like a mirror . . . a diz you will be really proud of.

My horn diz disappeared the first time I gave a demonstration of combing—it had proved irresistible to someone. But he repented, for it was returned anonymously a few weeks later, much to my delight.

The slot is easily made by drilling two $\frac{3}{16}$-inch (5 mm) holes at about $\frac{5}{16}$-inch (8 mm) centres, and sawing or filing away the material between them. Round and smooth off the edges and you have an attractive little tool.

The other requirements are some device with which you can accurately measure and apply oil to the fibre, and a water spray.

For my oiler I once again turned to my friend, the vet. He has disposable hypodermic syringes by the dozen; once used they are thrown away. These I find very good for the job. The only drawback is that the rubber plunger soon swells if you leave it in contact with the oil, so either wash it every time after use or get several plungers while you are on the scrounge, or, more expensive but better, buy a syringe with a ceramic plunger (Fig. 26).

My wife provided the water spray in the form of a pump-style atomizer that had previously been used for cosmetic purposes. It was particularly useful because it gave 1 ml of water at each pump (Fig. 27).

Chapter 2
Wool Sorting

In the days when hand wool combing flourished, the comber restricted his work to scouring, drying and combing. It was no part of his responsibility to determine what sort of fleece was used for a given yarn. The fleece was given to him ready sorted; he then prepared it for combing and returned it in the form of combed tops.

Our problems are a little more extensive, for, in addition to doing his work, we have to buy our fleeces and then separate out the various qualities of fibre they may contain. The fleece requirements of the worsted spinner are rather specialized; as a general rule, the staple should be in excess of 4 inches (10 cm). Shorter staple can still be combed but the yarns spun from them become increasingly whiskery, although it may be worth noting here that I find combing the shorter staple fleeces much faster than carding them, and that the worsted spun yarn produced is often mistaken for woollen spun because of its hairiness. It is, however, generally enhanced by the sheen which results from spinning combed fibre.

In the U.K. there are over 100 grades of fleece with a staple in excess of 4 inches. There are those fleeces traditionally used for combing, with very long staple and pronounced lustre, and many more with a staple suitable for combing, but which were probably not used by the specialists of old.

Because the long staple fleeces are grown mainly on the east coast of England, while I live in the far South-West, I started my wool combing with the fleeces I was able to obtain close to home. The staple was around 5 inches (13 cm) and it combed and spun beautifully; it was many years before I was able to obtain a traditional combing quality fleece. The staple was around 10 inches (25 cm) and it needed considerable practice before I was satisfied with the yarn I spun from it.

The shorter staple fleeces are rather more numerous, and consequently easier to obtain. They are considerably easier to comb and spin.

My advice then is to purchase a fleece or fleeces with a staple of around $5\frac{1}{2}$ inches (14 cm), but not in excess of 7 inches (18 cm). There are even a few of that length that exhibit some lustre, but if it is absent the yarn will still have the attractive sheen which is absent in woollen spun yarns.

I think that in the early stages of wool combing, it is important that the fleece you obtain should be repeatable year after year, and it would obviously be better to find a local supply of suitable fibre than to have to purchase it, unseen, from a distant source. You will find that combing and spinning medium staple can be learnt very quickly, and when a fair degree of competency has been reached, the longer staple may be experimented with. If you live in an area where only the longer staple fleeces are available, then I think I would strongly recommend you to go to the extra trouble of obtaining medium staple fleeces. Of course, you can learn from scratch on a long staple fleece—the apprentices of old must have done so—but the work is considerably harder, possibly discouragingly so.

Apart from the combing and spinning being easier with a medium staple fibre, the blending of fibres of similar length but of varying quality or colour is likely to be very much more thorough, as the total number of individual fibres involved in a yarn of given diameter increases. There will, of course, be twice as many 6-inch (15 cm) staple fibres in a given length of yarn as 12-inch (30·5 cm).

In the U.K., with the exception of the Shetland Isles, anyone owning more than four sheep is obliged to sell his fleeces to the British Wool Marketing Board. This has been so since that Board was created by Act of Parliament in 1950. So, unless you have a friend with a few sheep in his orchard, or live outside the U.K., it is to the Wool Marketing Board that you will have to make your legal application for a fleece.

So we will assume that you have obtained a fleece or fleeces with a staple of, say, $5\frac{1}{2}$ inches (14 cm). If you have purchased it in the U.K. from the Board, it will have been rolled up according to their instructions (Fig. 28) and can be unrolled by reversing the order.

Before you unroll the fleece, ensure that you have a large unimpeded floor space—linoleum or any smooth floor-covering is ideal. It must be efficiently and evenly illuminated. If the floor is dirty or oily, as the floor of a garage might be, then cover it with several layers of old newspapers upon which to spread your fleece. You can adopt the same procedure if the fleece has to be opened on the lawn.

The purpose of opening the fleece is to enable you to sort out the various qualities of fibre it may contain. Experience has shown that it is easier to do this as soon as possible after the fleeces have been shorn, than to store them and sort them one at a time as they are required. I think there are

THE RIGHT WAY TO ROLL A FLEECE

1
After clipping, lay out the fleece on a clean surface. flesh side down. (Blackface. Herdwick and Rough Fell fleeces should be laid flesh side up.) Pick off any extraneous matter, such as straw or twigs, and also remove any heavy, earthy bellies and daggs that may have been missed when trimming. Fold in the flanks towards the centre (as shown by dotted lines).

2
Turn in britch end and roll the fleece firmly and neatly towards the neck.

3
Draw out the wool at the neck end and twist slightly to form a rope or band of sufficient length to wrap round the rolled fleece. Do not twist this band too tightly or the wool may be damaged.

4
Pull the band tightly around the rolled fleece and tuck in the loose end. Make sure the fleece is firmly secured or it will soon become unrolled —and loose or unwrapped fleeces incur a price penalty.

Fig. 28 By reversing the U.K. Wool Marketing Board's instructions, the fleece is unrolled.

Fig. 29 Fleeces as delivered, rolled and tied.

two main reasons for this. One is that the longer the fleeces are stored, the stiffer the grease they contain becomes. This causes the locks to cling together and often makes opening the fleece difficult, to the extent that lumps of fibre may become detached from their original area, which may increase the uncertainties we all experience when we come new to sorting. The second reason is that once we have the 'feel' of the job and can begin to recognize the fibre variations, we might as well press on and sort all our fleeces while we have the floor space cleared. It is just as easy to store sorted as unsorted fleece.

It is the job of the wool sorter to divide the fleece into the various qualities of fibre it may contain; it is a highly specialized trade, demanding keen eyesight, extremely sensitive fingers and years of practice.

A boss sorter could divide a fleece into 14 or 16, to him, clearly definable qualities. You and I, with our fingers more accustomed to housework, gardening or other work, would probably find it difficult to classify 3 or 4 grades with any degree of certainty. Moreover, it is a job we can only experience once for each fleece we use and, since most of us will probably not spin more than a few fleeces in a year, it is going to take a very long time for us to improve our abilities in this direction.

That is not to say we should not try, but it *is* an admission that we cannot hope to do everything perfectly, that we must recognize that there are some skills so specialized that we are unlikely to acquire them within the limits of our available experience.

If that argument is acceptable, then we can conclude that for everyday run-of-the-mill work, the spinning of yarns for furnishings or for woven or knitted outer garment cloths, we can in all probability sort our fleece into two or three clearly distinguishable usable qualities; that for soft knitting wools we can, though with rather more waste, sort out the very soft fibres, but that if we desire a large quantity of yarn of one particular quality, we should probably be better advised to go to a stapler and purchase the fibre ready sorted, if that is at all possible.

We shall see later that there are some occasions when it is vitally necessary to sort the fleeces into staple length as well as into fibre quality, but that is relatively easy. It is the grading of the fibre that requires the greater skill.

The main point I want to make at this stage is that we can still produce first-class yarns designed for specific end uses by:

(a) perhaps being a little more wasteful in discarding any fibre from areas of the fleece traditionally accepted as being unsuitable;

37

(b) perhaps restricting our yarn requirements to match the fibre *we know we can sort*;

(c) going to a specialist sorter when yarns of a particular quality beyond our ability to sort the fibre are required.

When your fleece has been unrolled, it will resemble roughly the shape shown in Fig. 30, and you can begin to assess the varying qualities of fibre

Fig. 30   Unrolled fleece.

it contains. If you have a friend who has experience in sorting, I would strongly advise you to ask for some instruction, but, failing that, you must carry on and do the best you can, and you will be surprised at how good that can be.

Fig. 30(a)   Where changes in fibre quality might be expected—though varying considerably from breed to breed. An experienced sorter would determine grades within each area:

    a   Area over shoulders, most of back and sides—first quality fibre with even staple;

    b   Rump and haunches—coarser fibre;

    c   Areas of little use either through being fouled with manure or because fibres are short, or grey and kempy.

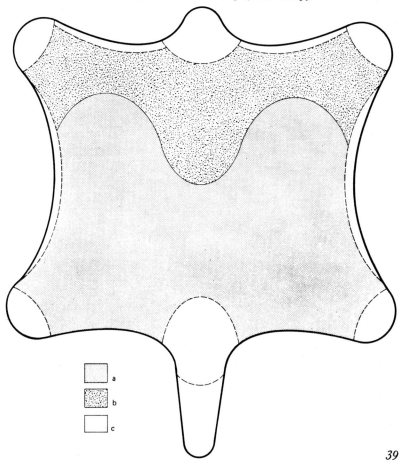

a

b

c

First of all, for any particular breed of sheep, there will be areas of the fleece where you can expect to find the better quality fibres, and other areas where, more often than not, the fibre is of little use. It is probable that some perceptible difference in the fibre can be detected roughly along the lines shown in Fig. 30(a), but before you go pulling away tufts of wool, remember that in doing so you will alter the appearance of the fleece, and the areas where quality change may be expected may become more difficult to define. So, before any fibre is removed, lay some cords over the fleece following the general lines of the diagram.

Having done that, we can now discard those areas stained with manure or caked with dirt—the britch and perhaps the extremities of the legs. You will observe that when you lay your hand flat on the fleece, it often causes a natural parting to appear between the locks. Always try to separate the pieces you wish to remove by opening out these natural partings. Do not just grab lumps of wool and pull, for that way you can divide the locks themselves where, as potential combers, we want to keep the locks intact until they are placed on the combs (Fig. 31).

It is unusual for the locks along the edge of either side of the fleece to be of much use to us. They are usually short, sometimes grey in appearance, and are best discarded. Grey fibre is regarded as difficult to dye, and is generally rather dull and lifeless. It may perhaps find some use among the short fibre users, but not for us. The head and neck area is often short or grey, or both, and can be discarded (Fig. 32).

Fig. 31   Always try to find a natural parting in the locks.

Fig. 32   Matted short grey fibre of little use for anything. Discard it.

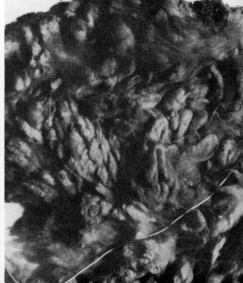

All the while you are poring over your fleece, keep a special watch for any very short fibres. There are usually two sorts, one caused when the shearer has left rather more wool on the sheep than he ought, and has had another go at it, thereby producing a small bundle of fibre anything up to 1 inch (25 mm) long. It will have the same colour and fineness of the main mass of the fleece, but will be very short. These we call *double-cuts*. The other is a short stubbly fibre, very coarse, often dead white, sometimes brownish red, and is called *kemp*. Kemp can be a long fibre too. It is dead in appearance, hairy, lifeless, and must always be discarded when ever it is seen.

Short kemp and double-cuts are a nuisance in worsted yarns. Because they are short, the ends do not fold in the yarn like those of other fibres, and the part which protrudes is often held rigid, making the finished fabric prick and irritate the skin. Always be ready to pounce on kemp and double-cuts at whatever stage of the operation they may be seen, whether it may be in the opening, the sorting, the scouring or the combing . . . remove them (Figs 33 and 34).

We are now left with that part of the fleece which covered the back of the sheep, down its sides and over its rump. Most often the softest, finest fibre can be expected over the shoulder areas. Frequently the area over the rump contains fibres which are coarse and hairy, so let us look for these coarser fibres first. They are fairly easy to distinguish for they lack the liveliness, the spring, of the better quality fibres; they often more resemble

Fig. 33 The short, thick white fibres spreading from the centre to the bottom left are kemp. They are clearly seen against the finer, softer wool fibres.

Fig. 34 Remove them wherever they are seen.

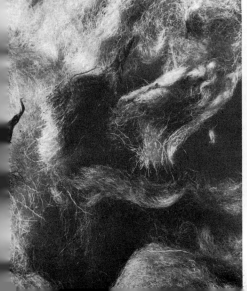

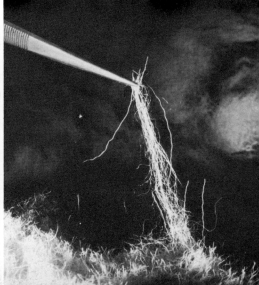

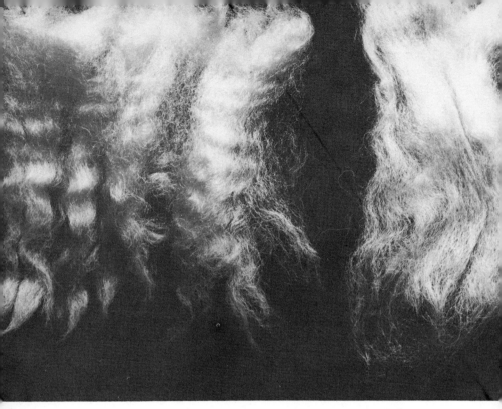

Fig. 35   It is easy to distinguish the coarser, long, hairy fibre (right) *from the soft, springy, lively fibre which we will call Grade I* (left).

hair than wool, and are usually larger in diameter, coarser in every way. Unfortunately, they are often amongst the longest fibres in the fleece, but, since they tend to spin into hard, lifeless yarn, we will remove them carefully from whatever area of the fleece they appear (Fig. 35).

The coarser fibres may not be very large in total quantity, but should be retained and spun into experimental yarns at a later date. It may be that some use can be found for the yarns they produce, where the lack of handle may not be important. If you are fortunate with your fleeces it may take several before a usable quantity of coarse fibre has accumulated.

It may now become increasingly difficult to tell the difference in the quality of the fibre which remains. For, quite apart from our lack of experience, in the U.K. the Wool Marketing Board, by its advocating selective breeding, is gradually eliminating or reducing the variations of fibre quality found within the fleece. If you can detect any difference in the

Fig. 36   The produc' of one fleece: Left back   *Grade I;* Left foreground   *Grade III, long and hairy;* Centre   *Grade II;* Right   *grey and short fibres, or fibres too contaminated to be usable.*

quality, the fineness, the handle, the springiness or lustre of the remaining fleece, if any area appears more live than another, then sort it out and call it Grade I, placing it in a separate box. What is left we can call Grade II, the coarse fibre Grade III (Fig. 36).

The bulk of the remaining fibre will probably be Grade II, but within both this and possibly the Grade I fibre, there may be some noticeable variation in the staple length. It will considerably improve the quality of our yarns if the grades can now be sub-divided into staple length. This is relatively easy, as the variations can be measured. Some fleeces yield a very uniform staple, while others contain considerable variation. If your fleece came from the Wool Board, it will have been selected for its uniformity, and you might find that in the whole fleece the variation is little more than one inch. However, if it is measurable, place the longer staple in one box, the shorter in another, but keeping the grades separate, of course (Fig. 36a).

Fig. 36(a)   Using the top of the pad as a convenient measure.

Sorting is a skill acquired by training and actually doing the job. Because of our complete lack of training we must do the best we can with the tools at our disposal—our hands, our eyes, and all the books on the subject we can find. We shall achieve greater perfection more quickly if we stick to one type of fleece, so that we can more easily recognize the fibres it contains and the areas where the quality changes can be expected. A permanent record will probably help in achieving uniformity in sorting, and a sketch plan/map of the fleece, showing where, from your own experience, you can expect the quality variations and what they are, will probably help the job along next year.

It is only from uniformity that quality will come. Uniformity of fleece leads to greater confidence in sorting, which in turn leads to a better ability to sort.

If you sort all your fleeces in one session, not only will the job be easier because the fleece will be fresh, but you will have an accurate idea of how much fibre you have in each of your grades. The graded fibre must be stored separately in sacks, boxes or bins, but never in sealed plastic bags. The dirty waste is thrown away and the very short fibres, those too short for combing, disposed of to a woollen spinner.

Chapter 3
To Scour or Not To Scour

While you are engaged in sorting, two characteristics of wool other than its fibrous nature will have become apparent to you. One is the smell which will have assailed your nose, and the other is the filth, the dirt plus grease or oil, that has accumulated on your hands.

There are two quite distinct schools of thought on what the next stage in the preparation of the fleece for spinning should be. One takes the fleece just as it is and either spins it direct from the locks or cards it, depending on the type of yarn required. The grease, the dirt, the smell, are all retained in the yarns produced and have to be removed at a later stage before the cloth produced from them can be worn, or the yarns or the finished cloth dyed.

The other method removes the grease, dirt and smell by scouring the fleece before it is spun.

I have not been able to determine when the idea that it was better to spin dirty fleece than clean fleece came about. Certainly it was after the end of commercial hand-spinning, and in all probability the practice crept back with the raising of the process from a trade to a craft in the mid-1800s. By now it is part of the mystique, the general esoteric heritage handed on from one generation of hand-spinners to the next without its origins ever being seriously questioned.

Phrases like 'The yarns are so much more elastic when spun in the grease', 'It is more thrifty to spin in the grease', or 'Fleece retaining its natural oil is much easier to spin' are all passed on as unquestionable truths, no-one ever troubling to test their validity.

Of course, it must be recognized that in some parts of the world fleeces grow during a season when rainfall is low, where sheep can graze over enormous areas, and the fleeces will inevitably be cleaner than our home-grown variety where mud and manure tend to soil the fibre.

Even so, some dirt is present and will be trapped in the fibres as they are twisted into a yarn.

Yet it is the grease that seems to occupy such an important part of the argument. It is the grease, we are told, which imparts the lovely soft, silky feel and enables you to spin such a fine yarn so easily. It does, too—there is no getting away from it.

The grease—the lanolin of soap, commerce and cosmetics—enables the fibres to slide past each other so that a constant fibre amount can be presented for twisting, resulting in a yarn of constant diameter.

It does it particularly well when the fleece is freshly shorn; of course, the ambient temperature is usually fairly high then, and that too affects the consistency of the grease.

Few of us, though, spin a whole fleece during the summer months. As winter approaches and the temperature drops, the grease gets progressively stiffer and the work gets harder because the fibres now cling together instead of slipping past each other. Spinsters have to adapt their touch to meet the changing characteristics of the raw material and, of course, re-acquire the light touch when the fresh fleeces arrive the following year.

Yarn spun from unscoured fleece must be scoured before it can be dyed. It seems reasonable to suppose that this scouring will be more difficult to achieve satisfactorily in fibres twisted together than in fibres not under compression. For the same reason, it would seem to follow that dye penetration and take-up may be less even than in un-spun fibres.

What then is the alternative? It is to scour the fleece before it is spun, to wash it, to remove all the dirt, the smell, the grease. Then, after drying, fresh clean oil is added and the fibre spun into a yarn. If coloureds are required, the fibre is dyed between the scouring and oiling stages. The dye penetration is unhindered by any compression of the fibres, and should, for any reason, some areas take the dye more readily than others, the carding or combing processes will even out the variations, producing an absolutely uniform colour.

The spinster can find new areas of interest; no longer need yarns be composed of just one colour, for by mixing or blending fibres of various colours, new and interesting shades emerge. For instance, 25% brown, 25% yellow and 50% white (un-dyed wool) produces a lovely old gold, while 25% brown and 75% white produces a smoky grey.

I must admit what must by now be fairly obvious—I am strongly in favour of scouring the fleece, because not only is it more pleasant to handle, but the spinner has greater flexibility in the use of the basic raw material. Because the spinner has a constant supply of clean, dry fleece, to which is added the required amount of oil immediately prior to spinning, the raw

46

material used has characteristics which are absolutely constant, month in, month out. Because the quality of the raw material never varies, touch need never vary and the chances of the yarn's being similarly uniform are considerably increased (see Colour Plate 1).

There is one other fact that clinched the matter for me. In all the descriptions of wool combing that have survived, observers are unanimous in stating that the fibre was scoured first. William Partridge, in his book (1823) *A Practical Treatise on the Dyeing of Woollen, Cotton and Skein Silk*, advocates scouring first . . . and so will we.

(One cannot help speculating on the effect that a lump of smelly, dirty fleece would have on the 'I spin in the grease' brigade, if they were not conditioned hand-spinners, were it dragged into their homes by the dog!)

Scouring the fleece is simplicity itself. Weigh out half-a-pound (226 g) of sorted wool and place it in a sink which has been filled with water heated to about 25–40°C (77–104°F), into which 2 oz (57 g) of soapflakes have been dissolved. Of course, the 2 oz of soapflakes will vary with the hardness of the water in your area, either more or less being required. Gently push the fleece under the suds and leave it. I have never worked in a hard water area, but rather than use softeners, I think I would try to gather rainwater. (Plate 2.)

When the water has cooled, or after, say, two or three hours, drain it out, squeeze the fleece to the side of the sink, lift it out and prepare a second sink full of suds.

If the fleece was not too dirty, this second immersion, leaving it over-night, will probably suffice; very dirty fleeces may require a third wash. I have only ever had one that did.

I used to like to arrange the second washing overnight because, not only did it reduce the temptation to stir the fleece about to see how things were progressing, but I was also less likely to receive complaints from the commissariat to 'get that dirty stinking mess out of my kitchen'. In fact, since our early days, we have had a two-bowl stainless steel sink installed in our dyehouse, which makes the job much easier. The last soapy wash from one batch of fibre can, by adding some hot water, be used for the first soak of the next batch, thus effecting some slight economy, which might be important if rainwater is being used.

We always use soapflakes, by the way. I have no doubt at all that many of the commercially available detergents would work quite as well, but I have never been able to obtain any information from research organizations on what effect they have on the fibre, so I decided to leave them alone. We

47

buy our soapflakes in bulk as it is cheaper that way. It does a near-perfect job and at least one can have confidence that, since the formula for soap-flakes does not seem to change, the results of the steeping will be constant.

To return to the batch of fibre that has been soaking overnight; drain away the soapy water, squeeze or press the fleece against the side of the bowl or sink, and lift it out before the rinse water is admitted. If you have an old spin-drier, it will extract the sudsy water very efficiently and make rinsing that much more efficient. Two or three rinses in fresh water, with a spin between each, will usually ensure a creamy-white, sweet-smelling fleece which will be a joy to handle.

Avoid handling the fleece more than is necessary while it is in the water—resist the temptation to stir it around; lift it clear of the sink when the bowl is filling, so that the water swirl does not tangle the fibres, and, as I said, time things so that the main wash occurs overnight.

I usually wash the whole fleece, half-a-pound at a time, until it is all clean, keeping the previously sorted qualities separate, of course.

All the foregoing is related to a fairly normal, averagely dirty fleece, where the locks are stiff with grease and dirt, but not clogged or matted together or caked solid with mud.

The more matted or dirty the fleece, the longer will the soakings have to be, and you might find soaking for a couple of days in plain water advantageous. The most difficult fleece I ever had to wash was a Lincoln with a 9-inch (23 cm) staple. The locks were caked solid with mud, and it proved necessary to soak each batch for three days in cold water before the mud was soft enough to be washed out, and then there followed countless changes of water before the fleece appeared clean. On that sort of occasion, guide lines have to be bent, and it was found necessary to knead the fleece in the sink in order to dislodge the mud. Some felting of the fibre is, of course, inevitable, which makes the subsequent combing harder work.

Drying can take a surprisingly long time, and it must be emphasized that the fleece must be quite dry before it is stored, to avoid any danger of moulds growing on the fibres. A spin-drier is a boon for removing most of the free water quickly. If the only spin-drier available is that which is used for the household wash, or part of a combined washing machine, be sure to place the fleece in a large muslin bag before spinning, to avoid any danger of locks fouling the extractor pump. Remember to distribute the mass evenly within the drier before switching on.

If you have no spin drier, the fleece can be folded inside an old sheet and mangled, or the sheet can be twisted to wring out most of the water, but

Fig. 37 A support of wire netting allows the fleece to be hung out in the fresh air but prevents it all from blowing away.

that is a job for two persons unless you can anchor one end of the sheet firmly.

For final drying, we made a support from 1-inch (2·5 cm) mesh wire netting, which we hang up in a current of fresh air on the clothes line. The fleece is pushed through the mesh in a number of places, enabling the wool to be spread out thinly over a large area without its all blowing away. I repeat, washed fleece should not be stored until quite dry. Damp fibre will soon start to smell faintly of mildew (Fig. 37).

Some of you may take encouragement from the fact that I can sort a clean or scoured fleece far more easily than one which is dirty. This is a natural skill which I acquired by use. I am continually handling clean fibre for combing and spinning, and I can tell from the look of it, the feel of it, which sort of quality it conforms to in my scale. So my own method has evolved to suit my own skills—or lack of them.

I first open out the fleece and, following the guide lines, sort it into the rough generalities of grades, after having removed all the unwanted parts and all the kemp I can see.

49

I then scour each batch separately and after it is dry I find I am able to discard unsuitable fibres with much more confidence than when the fleece was full of dirt and grease. As I said, it is a question of use. The professional sorter sees nothing but unscoured fleece and develops skills specially for that raw material, so it is not unreasonable to suppose that those of us who habitually handle scoured fleece should be able to sort it more easily in that state.

It is at this stage that a decision must be taken as to whether the fibre will be dyed before spinning, if coloured yarns are required, or whether the yarns will be dyed.

On this question of dyeing, prejudice runs as strongly as on the question of spinning in the grease, and is really indicative of the rather 'dyed-in-the-wool' attitude many of us have towards change. I have given my opinions and methods in Chapter 5, which is devoted to the preparation of dyed yarns.

To summarize, for worsted yarns we require a quantity of long staple wool fibre, which has been sorted into grades according to fibre quality and staple length, and which has been scoured and dried.

Chapter 4
First Steps in Combing

In the days of the professional worker, wool combing called for a pair of wool combs, a pad, a diz, oil, water, a supply of fibre, and a stove upon which to heat the combs.

With the addition of a pair of scales, just about the same equipment will be required today. Having made the combs, pad and diz, the only remaining difficulty will be the method of heating the combs.

Heating

First of all, why heat them at all? Well, heating the combs always helps the job along; the fibre mass becomes more supple as the heat is transferred from the tines to the fibre and to the oil and water retained by it.

In really warm weather, it is often possible to comb without raising your tools above the ambient temperature, but in colder weather the oil tends to accumulate on the tines, which become tacky, causing fibres to cling to them, adding considerably to the effort required in passing the comb through the fibre mass. Heating effectively prevents that happening.

For heating, the combers of old used a stove called locally a 'pot o' four', possibly derived from the French *pot au feu*; it seems that it could be used by up to four workers simultaneously. As you can see from Fig. 38, it had a flat top above which was supported an iron plate. The combs were slipped in between the two to warm the tines. This was sometimes done when the comb was loaded with fibre, which was pushed to the head of the comb so that it fell down the outside of the stove.

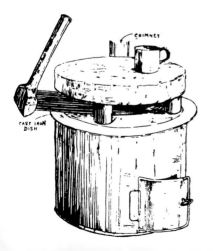

Fig. 38   Illustration of the Woolcomber's 'Pot o' four' from Hand Woolcombing *by H. Ling Roth. The pot could be used by up to four people, but some preferred to work alone. Thus an independent person was, within living memory, often referred to as a 'poto' one'.*

Those of you with cooking stoves of the solid fuel type and with a hot-plate can use these quite effectively. Perhaps I should mention that it is never necessary to heat the combs when they are loaded when working in the warmth of your home.

Always protect the head of your comb from the heat of the stove by placing a folded oven cloth under it. The tines should be resting on the hot-plate with the lid resting on them. (See Fig. 39.)

Remember, when we talk about heating the combs we really mean warming them, no more. Just too hot to hold comfortably—not glowing!

Those of you who rely on gas or electricity will have slightly more trouble.

I have always insisted that the combs *must not be laid directly on a gas or electric ring*. I think this is highly dangerous.

It is far better to place a pan of water on the ring, of sufficient size to enable about two-thirds of the tine area to be submerged, heat the water to around boiling and rest the tines in that. It works perfectly and is far quicker and safer than any other method (Fig. 40).

The combs stay warm for a surprisingly long time, because, I imagine, of the insulating qualities of the fibre with which they are loaded.

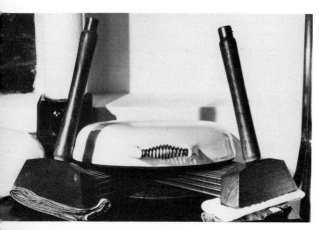

Fig. 39   Combs warming on a solid fuel cooker. Note pads under comb heads to protect them from direct contact with the stove.

Fig. 40   Method employed for gas or electric stoves ensures rapid heating with complete safety.

Oil

We have mentioned several times that oil must be added to the scoured fleece before it can be spun—or indeed before it can be carded or combed. It must be clean oil, of course, which will help to return the fleece to the soft, supple state it was in before scouring.

But how much oil—and of what type? History is not a lot of help, for few records exist which specify either the type of oil or the quantity, and those that do are concerned with the woollen trade, not worsted. The best that researchers have been able to do regarding the oils used for wool combing is to compare the stocks carried by oil chandlers in the textile and non-textile producing areas and see if any pattern was discernible.

From these comparisons it seems possible that wool combers used lard oil (made from pig fat), olive oil, palm oil, train oil (whale oil), Gallipoli oil (fermented olive oil), and fish oil. Rancid butter has also been mentioned as a possibility.

Today we have several new vegetable oils in addition to those already mentioned. We have maize oil, sunflower oil, corn oil, and a variety of blends of cooking oil. So I tried the lot!

I cannot truthfully say that I found any great difference in their properties as a lubricant for combing and spinning wool. Some were stiffer to use than others, some smelt more than others, one or two imparted their smell to the spun yarn to such an extent that it was almost impossible to remove it.

So I made a chart of desirable and undesirable qualities. At the head of the list of desirables was olive oil, and as it also came bottom on the list of undesirables, we have used it ever since. It lubricates well, has a pleasant aroma which, with the oil, is easily removed from the finished yarn and is kind to the skin.

Its main drawback is that it has a fairly high melting point and so is inclined to stiffen when the ambient temperature drops to around the 10°C (50°F) mark, but this it has in common with many of the vegetable oils.

It is, though, considerably more expensive than some of the other vegetable oils but, as we shall see, the quantity required is so small that the cost, spread over the amount of fibre a pint of olive oil will lubricate, is negligible. You might be interested to know that it is usually still possible to purchase it in half-gallon cans.

Quantity

As far as I am aware, the quantity of oil to be applied to scoured fibre for hand wool combing and subsequent hand-spinning has never been stated. Contemporary statements say 'apply a little oil', or 'sprinkle on a few drops of oil', and that is the nearest we get.

This seemed rather haphazard to me, and so we set out to apply carefully measured amounts of oil to carefully weighed quantities of wool.

As you might expect, very small amounts of oil have no apparent effect on the behaviour of the fibres; in combing they fuzz out, hang up and are difficult to handle. They are harsh to the touch and comb with a dry rasping sound. More oil tends to smooth things down a little, the fibres slip past each other more easily, and the harsh sound of dry combing disappears.

More oil may make the process easier still, but it is a strange fact that once the level of easy working has been reached the addition of still more oil does not help the process at all—it just makes it more messy. Remember, excess of oil is not only wasteful of an expensive commodity, but also means greater difficulty in the final scouring.

Finally we adopted 6 millilitres of olive oil to 40 g of scoured fibre as a standard (4·25 ml to 1 oz).

This works out at:

> 6 ml to 40 g = standard comb
> 4·5 ml to 30 g = medium comb
> 3 ml to 20 g = small comb.

The only reference to the actual quantity of oil used in the days of the hand textile trade that I found is that given by William Partridge, writing about the woollen trade in 1823. He advocated from 2 to 3 lb (1–1·4 kg) of oil spread over 20 lb (9 kg) of wool. You can imagine that when I weighed 6 ml of olive oil and found that 6 ml to 40 g works out at 2·77 lb to 20 lb of wool, I was rather pleased.

As already mentioned, a hypodermic syringe is ideal as an oil applicator; the quantity is easily seen and the needle causes the oil to emerge in small droplets which can be sprinkled evenly over the fibre mass.

Water

We often read that combers added water to their fibre in an endeavour to increase their earnings, since they were paid by weight. The water was squirted on to the fibre during the combing process from the mouth—a method which requires considerable practice before anything like a fine spray can be produced. A few poorly aimed jets decided me that a more modern approach was called for, and so I purchased a small pressurized garden spray, which ejects a veritable mist and is just right for the job. Soon after, my wife gave me a discarded cosmetic spray which works just as well—better in a way, for it works on a plunger pump principle, squirting out a millilitre of water each time.

Since no explanation other than the weight bonus is ever given for the water application, I omitted it from my combing without any detrimental effect that I could discern. Until, that is, we had a spell of crisp, cold, dry weather, when the friction of the warm combs through the fibre and the inter-fibre friction generated considerable static electricity. Tiny sparks would jump, to the accompaniment of a faint crackle. The effect on the fibre was spectacular in the extreme. Instead of forming the usual goatee beard shape I had come to expect, it all fluffed out like a feather duster, each of the fibres trying to get as far away from its neighbour as possible.

It was obvious that producing a fine sliver was going to be impossible, and since static is not generated in humid weather, I sprayed the fibre on the comb with water, with the result that the static was completely eliminated.

Since I believe it to be important for constant quality that the fibre we spin should always present the same characteristics to the fingers of the spinster, I dampen all the fibre all the time. In summer, in winter, whether static is likely or whether it is not. The effort is slight and the cost of water, in this process, is the least of our worries. It means that static simply never occurs, but that your fibre has the same feel that it would have if you applied water only when static was likely, which in the northern hemisphere can be any time from early October to late April or May. I use the same quantity of water as of oil.

I have often wondered whether the English combers of old added water for the same reason. After all, conditions giving rise to static must have been very frequent in the cold dry atmosphere of the east side of England.

Of course, the water would have added a weight bonus, but it would have been a bonus of necessity, at least during the cold, dry winter months and fresh, frosty spring mornings. It is an intriguing thought—neither would it have been the first time historians have placed the wrong interpretation on a known fact.

Scales

A really good balance is necessary if quantities of fibre are to be weighed accurately. I have a strong prejudice against the common clock-dial spring balance, much preferring the type working on a fulcrum, a true balance in fact.

My experience has been that it is very difficult to buy a pair of scales for ordinary household use today, and finally, since I couldn't buy what I wanted, I had to make it. The balance illustrated is the result. It took ten hours to make, from scraps of wood, iron and welding rod I had about the workshop. It is far more sensitive than the kitchen scales I used previously. It has, as you can see, an easily-read pointer by which an exact reading can be obtained, but the main feature applicable to our work is that the pan measures about $9\frac{1}{2} \times 13\frac{1}{2}$ in (24×34 cm), giving ample space for the rather bulky material we shall be weighing (Figs 41 and 42).

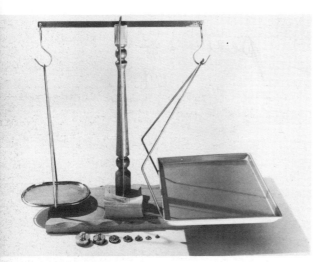

Fig. 41 An accurate balance made in 10 hours' work from odd scraps of metal and wood. The pan is a shallow baking dish, the pan support made for easy access. The weights were purchased.

Fig. 42 The balance. The short bar under the left-hand pan support compensates for the difference in weight of the two pans.

You will notice, too, that the pan rests on a platform suspended from one side only, giving unhindered access for loading and unloading. I only wish I had made them years ago!

That pair of scales was made especially for weighing fibre for oiling, combing and blending. You will need another pair for weighing bulk fibre for scouring, dyeing or weighing out total quantities for blending. For this a large spring balance of the baby-weighing variety will probably serve. I use an old balance of the suspended type; for pans I use plastic wash bowls. In use, the balance is suspended from a beam or a nail driven in a door lintel, when it can be used in the open doorway. It is an easy type to make, and will be quite accurate enough for large quantities of fibre. Suspend it so that there is about 8 in (20 cm) clearance under the bowls, and you will find it very easy to use (Fig. 42a).

Fig. 42(a)   Old balance, with plastic bowls added for pans, used for weighing out bulk fibres.

Weights

I was brought up to use avoirdupois. I dislike change, and clung in desperation to the world I knew. I know now what a fool I've been! The metric system, for the work we are undertaking, could hardly be bettered. The yarns we shall produce composed of blended fibres will have their composition stated in grammes, 50 g white, 30 g yellow, 10 g brown, 10 g green—but imagine converting that to avoirdupois for a 1-oz comb load!

But of course, if you prefer working with avoirdupois, or are unable to obtain metric weights, a compromise must be found. The main snag is that often a half-ounce is the smallest weight supplied with a balance, and our need is for much smaller divisions than that. It is here that you have to depart from commercial weights and make your own.

At first I tried coins of the realm, but it wasn't too satisfactory, and then I tried small metal washers, with much greater success. Eventually I found some that weighed 20 to the 1 oz, and then I was able to work in percentages without much trouble. Thus, if we require 50% white, 30% yellow, 10% brown and 10% green in the whole fibre mass to be spun, and we get that percentage correct in each successive comb-load, it will be correct for the whole. Those percentages translated into washers would be: 10 washers of white, 6 washers of yellow and 2 washers each of brown and green.

I drove a nail into a block of wood, and use it as a washer spike to retain the weights, much like the old-fashioned letter spikes.

Staple Length

Worsted spinners always prefer the longer staples, for the longer the staple, the fewer the ends in a given length of yarn, and the more thready and smooth the yarn is likely to be. It is, too, only in the long combing quality wools that the pronounced lustre is found.

That does not mean that only long staple fibres can be spun. Our local sheep have a staple of between four and five inches, but it combs out into a lovely yarn. True, it has more ends sticking out of it than if spun from a longer staple, consequently the yarn is more whiskery in appearance, but it has all the other characteristics of a true worsted.

The beginner may, in fact, find that a shorter staple is easier to learn to spin than a longer staple would be, because, although the twist may influence and hold the same total number of fibres, the effect of the twist is restricted to a smaller area which is proportional to the fibre length.

The blending of fibres, either to achieve a desired shade of colour, or to intermingle fibres of different qualities or staple, also seems slightly more thorough with medium staple fibre.

There is another aspect, slightly more important to the spinner/weaver than to the spinner/knitter, and that is that the medium staple fleeces can be both combed and carded. The weaver then has the choice of, say, worsted warp and woollen weft.

Of course, even with a combing quality fleece there is a percentage of short fibre which is retained on the combs, the noils. This, too, is usable by carding and woollen spinning, but the quantity will be rather less than with shorter staple fleeces.

I think that a 3-inch (7·6 cm) staple might prove difficult to spin into a worsted yarn, but anything from four inches upwards can be combed to produce a yarn showing many of the worsted characteristics, but certainly retaining the main ones of sheen, smoothness (as compared with the same fibre carded), and strength.

It will be appreciated that these remarks are particularly intended for the person who has to make the best of whatever fleece he can obtain, not the person who has access to the fleece of his choice.

First Steps in Combing

Always bear in mind that you are going to produce a yarn in which the fibres are parallel, that the whole process is aimed at keeping the fibres parallel, and that since the fibres grow from the skin of the sheep parallel to one another, if we can preserve that state of affairs it will help our end product (Fig. 43).

Fig. 43   A general view of the woolcomber's bench—heated comb on the pad, weighed and oiled locks of wool ready for 'lashing on', oil bottle, water spray, scales and bulk fibre supply all ready to hand.

Since the combs take a little while to warm up, although they will warm instantly if you use the pan of near-boiling water technique, it is as well to place them to warm while the fibre preparation is going on.

Do remember that, while the bottom third of the tines can be hot, the heat must not be allowed to run up into the wooden head of the comb. The danger is that the wood will become charred and the tines will loosen. The combs I use were made eight years ago in the manner I have explained and, with the exercise of care, are still as sound as the day they were made.

With the combs warming and the pad securely fixed, we can proceed with the weighing.

Take the very greatest care with your weighing, always. Remember that we are striving for quality; we want to repeat the process ounce after ounce after ounce.

We can only obtain a uniform product if the process is uniform. We *must* start with exactly the same amount of fibre in each batch, we *must* add the same quantity of oil, we *must* add the same quantity of water. Near enough is *not* good enough. If you are slipshod to start with your yarns will be slipshod in character.

So we will start by weighing out an exact quantity of fibre. The comfortable load for the large comb illustrated is 40 g, which I find I can wield all day without getting unduly tired. The medium comb holds 30 g, and 20 g is right for the small combs (see also table on p. 17).

Lay the bulk fibre down on the bench, and although it looks a homogeneous mass you will see, if you part the locks carefully, that there are probably natural thin places where the mass will part fairly easily. Always try to use these partings for separating the locks if you can (Fig. 44).

Fig. 44 *Try to pull out the locks cleanly along a natural parting—do you see the lump of double-cut near the index finger of the right hand. Remove it!*

Try to pull out the locks so that they come away cleanly without dragging half an adjacent lock away with them. If you hold the fibre mass down with the flat of one hand, leaving a tuft or two of locks standing clear, you will be able to pull out the locks by grasping them individually by the tips. Sometimes, indeed often, a group of three or four locks becomes detached; just leave them as they are and lay them on the scales with the single locks. When a comb-load (40 g in this case) has been weighed, the locks are removed from the scales pan and laid in line on the bench, the hide ends (butts) all facing towards the rear, the tips towards the edge. If you see any obvious blemishes—double cuts, kemp, etc.—lift them out before the lock is weighed, of course, or indeed whenever they are seen.

With the locks in line and bunched together, the oil can be applied, sprinkled in fine droplets evenly over the fibres. Now follow with the same quantity of water and we are just about ready (Figs 45 and 46).

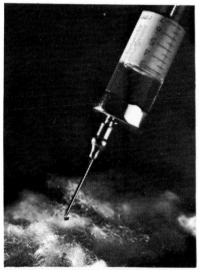

Fig. 45   6 ml of oil evenly distri-buted followed by . . .

Fig. 46   . . . 6 ml of water.

Take one of the heated combs and place it, tines vertical, on the pad and secure it with the peg.

Now, one lock at a time, place the fibre on the comb, keeping the butt on the tines, the tip end hanging free. Only place about the last half-inch (1·5 cm) over the tines, just enough to hold the lock securely in place (Fig. 47).

Although now we talk about placing the locks on the comb, and, being new to the game, we tend to do it carefully, later as we gain more confidence we shall flick on the lock with a twist of the wrist. Hence, this stage of the process was called 'lashing on'—a lovely phrase, I think.

Load the comb evenly; push the locks about halfway down the tines and spread them about so that the comb is evenly covered from side to side (Fig. 48).

Fig. 47 'Lashing on'—about ½-in (12 mm) of the lock is flicked over the front row of tines and drawn about ⅔ of the way down the comb.

Fig. 48 Comb loaded with 40 g of fibre prior to turning on its side to the combing position.

When the comb is loaded with the full 40 g of fibre, turn it on its side and secure it with the peg so that it will not pull out of the pad. Being left-handed, I turn my comb to the left—you might prefer it turned to the right. Use it whichever way comes naturally and make your pad right or left handed to suit. Take the second comb, which should by now be warm enough, and gently, with a steady chopping action, pass the hand-held comb through the tips of the fibres on the stationary comb. Some fibre will be pulled out of the locks and will cling to the moving comb. Make it a steady swinging chop which goes right down through the fibre. Not one which ends with the tines still in the fibre and has to be pulled away horizontally. Make your comb move in a circular motion. (See Fig. 49.) Figures 50 and 51 show the comb just entering and leaving on the first passage.

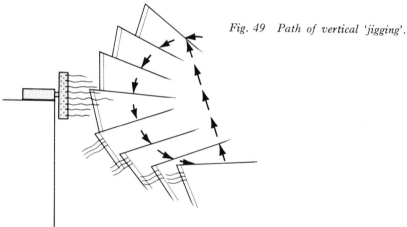

Fig. 49   Path of vertical 'jigging'.

Fig. 50   The fixed comb on its side, the moving comb just entering the tip of the locks.

Fig. 51   Nearing completion of the downwards stroke, with a small amount of fibre adhering to the moving comb.

Fig. 52 'Jigging' well advanced; most of the fibre has
been transferred from the
fixed to the moving comb.

Fig. 53 The sideways swinging
stroke which combs the fibre that
has accumulated on the hand comb
—and transfers it back on to the
fixed comb again.

Fig. 54 Sideways swing.

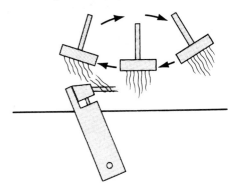

Keep on with the chopping motion—the professionals called this stage
'jigging'—gradually edging the comb deeper and deeper into the fibre mass.

More and more fibre will catch on to that already adhering to the moving
comb, until by the time the tines are nearly touching, the quantities on each
comb may be very similar. However, more fibre will gradually transfer to
the moving comb and, when the fixed comb has lost the greater part of its
load, the next stage commences (Fig. 52).

The fibre on the moving combs has now to be combed. This is accomplished by swinging the comb horizontally past the fixed comb, allowing
the tips of the fibre to come in contact with the tines of the stationary comb
as they pass, edging the swinging comb nearer the fixed unit with each
successive pass (Figs 53 and 54).

It has to be admitted that this sideways movement is rather more tiring,
more productive of aches, than the chopping motion, but you will be
surprised at how quickly you get used to it.

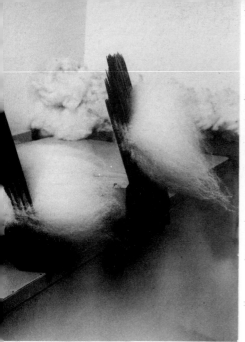

Fig. 55 Stop the combing when each comb holds a roughly similar amount of fibre.

Fig. 56 Smooth the fibres into a cone.

Carry on combing until the bulk of the fibre is transferred to the fixed comb again . . . and then start all over again with the chopping motion, repeating the process until the fibres are open and untangled, in the shape of a goatee beard, with the fibres in a parallel, orderly mass.

When this stage has been reached, stop the combing about halfway through either a chopping or a swinging phase, when each comb should contain roughly the same amount of fibre (Fig. 55).

Place the hand comb on the bench and turn the fixed comb to its vertical position, securing it with the retaining peg.

Smooth the fibre into a cone shape and, pinching the point (Fig. 56) between finger and thumb, gently draw off the fibres. After about 2 inches (5 cm) have been pulled out, pinch the beard again with the other hand near the tip, and draw out another couple of inches; then let go the first piece drawn and use that hand to pinch the fibre again, leap-frogging hand over hand, as a continuous sliver of fibre is drawn away from the comb.

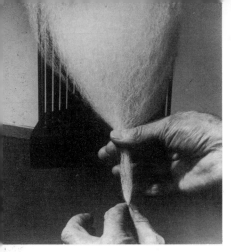 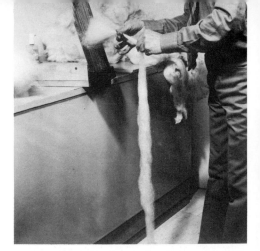

Fig. 57 *Pinch top and bottom with one hand, side to side with the other, leap-frogging hand over hand as the fibre is drawn off.*

Fig. 58 *Aim for a sliver about 2 in wide and ½-in thick (50 × 18 mm) when uncompressed.*

I have found that if you pinch the fibre top and bottom with one hand, and side to side with the other, a more general gather of fibres over the comb surface is maintained. Pinching in one plane only often results in a thinning of the centre of the cone, which, when the edges or sides of the comb load are finally gathered in, produces a sliver dense at the edges but thin in the centre. A pinch every two inches or so, especially with medium staples, produces a very even sliver, particularly in the final combings (Fig. 57).

The object is now to draw off the fibre in an orderly parallel state in a continuous unbroken sliver. It does not matter very much if this one does break, but if it does lay it down on the bench in the direction from which it came from the comb, so that you can tell which end came away from the comb first. Aim for a sliver about 2 inches wide and ½ inch thick (50 × 18 mm) when uncompressed (Fig. 58).

This is because if you do manage to unload the comb in a continuous sliver it must then be parted in about 3-foot lengths (1 m), which are laid side by side with the fibres flowing in the same direction. This was called 'planking' (Figs 59 and 60).

This is necessary because the drawing off tends to concentrate all the longer fibres in the first part, the shorter fibres coming off last; putting them side by side (planking them) evens things up a little (Fig. 61).

66

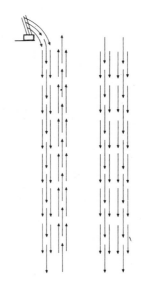

Fig. 59 Planking — laying
the sliver in about 3-ft (1-m)
lengths with the fibre flow in
in the same direction.

Fig. 61 How the direction of
the fibre flow is altered when
the sliver is planked end to
end (left), and end to severed
end of first half.

Fig. 60 Planking.

Fig. 62 'Noils'—the dross and short fibres held back by the comb; the quantity is small, so I discard it.

When I first started combing, I used to part the sliver in the centre and end-to-end it. There is no doubt at all that the staple length gets evenly distributed in that way. The disadvantage is that, if you imagine the fibres being drawn off in a continuous stream, the fibres will all be flowing in one direction, but if we end-to-end it, we get half the fibres flowing in one direction and half flowing in the opposite direction.

It seems better to keep the fibre flow all in one direction if at all possible, which necessitates the sliver being halved and the second half carried forward alongside the first, as in the diagram. The staple mix may not be quite so good, but the fibres, all flowing in the same direction, seem to me to twist into a smoother yarn than when end-to-ended. But the greatest help of all is to have a uniform staple in the first place. Even then, planking must never be omitted; 3-feet (1-m) lengths give a very even fibre distribution.

When most of the fibre has been drawn off from the comb you will see small lumps of fluff, pills and double cuts, seeds, etc. start to be drawn out from between the tines. *That* is the sign that enough fibre has been drawn off. Pull the sliver away and plank it in about 3-feet lengths.

Remove the waste from the comb (the noils) and put the comb back on the stove to warm. If you open out the waste and hold it up to the light,

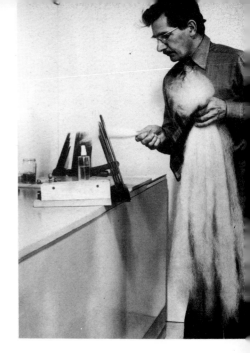

Fig. 63   The accumulated sliver from both combs is lashed on for a second combing. This time the fibre is held by all the rows of tines.

you will see that it is composed of a tangled mass of short fibres, lumps of fluff, etc. If you can find a use for it, all well and good, but I never have, except as a source of pills for fancy yarns, especially after coloured fibres have been combed. It comprises on average about 5% of the fleece, and so is perhaps worth experimenting with. My neighbours use most of my waste fleece for filling cushions and soft toys (Fig. 62).

Now fix the moving comb on the pad and draw off the fibre it contains, trying always to produce an even and continuous sliver. When the grot starts to pull out with the last few strands of fibre, part if off and plank it with the sliver drawn off from the first comb, ensuring that the fibre flow lies in the same direction in both

This first combing we will call the 'straightening' combing.

With the first comb freshly warmed and back on the pad, and the hand comb warming, we can take the two lots of sliver and lash them on to the static comb. Take the slivers in one hand; they will have the appearance of a lovely fluffy mare's tail. Holding them about nine inches from the tip, draw the end off by pulling firmly with the other hand. Aim for a tuft of about 7 to 9 inches (18–23 cm) of fibre. With a flick of your wrist, lash the tuft well on to the static comb, not just over the front tines as we did with the locks (Fig. 63).

We want this second jigging further to comb out the fibre mass, and unless it is firmly held, it will all pull off in a lump. So lash on the tufts so that they are held by all the rows of tines. If you get too enthusiastic and overshoot the tines, to the extent that most of the fibre is sticking out through the back row, then draw the tuft forward until its rear fibres are level with the back row of the tines.

As you pull out tufts with one hand, you will have to lower the other further and further down the diminishing length of sliver, until all the fibre is again on the static comb, which is then turned on its side.

Take the warmed second comb and start the chopping action again, taking care to engage only the tips of the fibres to start with. Even so, rather large lumps of fibre may pull away and may not seem to be firmly attached to the hand comb, but provided they do not fall off the next chop will push them on a bit further, and gather a little more fibre as well.

Soon most of the fibre will have been transferred to the hand comb and the swinging action can now be started. Transfer the fibre with the swinging or chopping action from one comb to the other twice, three or even four times until the mass is open and soft, until no lumps or blemishes appear in the fibre you can see.

At this point, stop the combing when each comb holds a roughly equal amount of fibre, lay the hand comb aside and raise the fixed comb vertical again. I find that if you just stop combing at the end of either a chopping or a swinging phase, the fibres on the collecting comb tend to be a little compacted, and that just one or two passes in the other direction—a swing or a chop as the case may be—opens them out again and eases the drawing off.

The goatee beard should be quite pronounced now, and just a gentle smoothing should produce a well-defined cone of fibre.

Now take the diz and, with the curved side facing the comb, pass the tip of the beard through the slot.

You will probably observe that because of the width of the comb and the combing action, the fibre mass extends more horizontally than vertically—so keep the diz horizontal.

You will see that the curved surface acts as the cone of a funnel, guiding the fibres into the slot. Whether that was the reason or not for using a piece of cow horn, I do not know, but the fact remains that it does the job exceptionally well, so one cannot help speculating how that particular material came to be used.

It is unfortunate that there is not an actual description of any one using

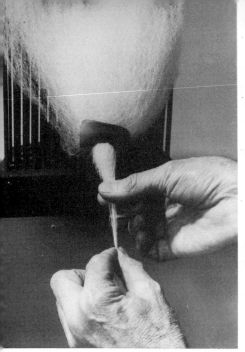
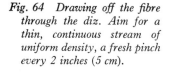

Fig. 64 *Drawing off the fibre through the diz. Aim for a thin, continuous stream of uniform density, a fresh pinch every 2 inches (5 cm).*

Fig. 65 *The diz jammed on the cone compresses the fibre in the slot, making it easier to control the quantity drawn off—though much harder work.*

the diz, for there are two distinct methods that I have discovered. What accounts there are just tell us that the fibre was drawn off through a diz. But you can either have it loose, supported by the tip of the cone, when it acts more as a funnel to guide the fibres into the slot, or you can jam it up on to the cone, when it serves both to guide and compress the fibres into the slot (Figs 64 and 65).

I started off using it as a guide, but now I use it to compress the fibres as well as guide them. I find that the resultant sliver is more uniform in density.

However, since the compressed fibres require considerably more effort to draw them out, we will start with the diz suspended from the tip, with the tip of the beard protruding through the slot. Now pinch the fibres and gently draw them away from the diz, which may tend to move out with them, so before you pinch the fibres with the other hand, push it up on the cone again. Remember to pinch top and bottom with one hand and

71

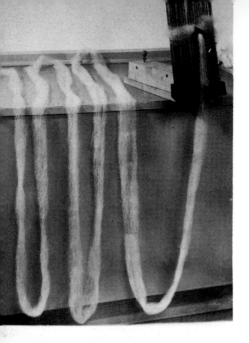

Fig. 66   About 20 feet of unbroken sliver from one comb load of 20 g fibre.

side to side with the other, drawing out a fine gossamer-like sliver about two inches at each draw. Soon it will reach the floor; let it fold backwards and forwards upon itself as you continue to draw out the fibre. Aim for an uncompressed sliver about 1½–2 in (3·5–5 cm) wide and ⅛ in. (3 mm) thick (Fig. 66).

If some of the fibres towards the comb edges seem reluctant to join their fellows, smooth them into the general fibre mass. Carry on drawing off till once again unwanted material in the shape of pills starts to appear. At that point, part the sliver. These noils can be retained and united with the next batch of straightened fibre to be combed.

In the days of the professional hand-spinner, the combed sliver was made first into a top, and then into a roving.

A top is a collection of slivers wound into a convenient shape for storage and/or transportation. This was necessary because wool combing was one trade and hand-spinning another and it was rare for a comber to spin his own fibre.

A roving is made by lightly twisting a sliver to form a thick, soft rope. The twist coils the fibre together and, as the roving is attenuated in the spinning process, the twist it contains tends to condense the fibres at the point where they are drawn out (drafted), making it easy for fresh fibres to be caught up as they are required.

Fig. 67   Finding the centre and planking an 18 ft (5.5 m) sliver. This time the sliver is parted in the centre and the end drawn off last joined to the severed end of the first half—the fibre will then all flow in the same direction.

It *is* possible to spin direct from a sliver, but it is far more difficult and the yarn is rather more hairy than when the sliver is twisted into a roving and then spun.

A roving is made by inserting twist into the sliver after it has been planked (Fig. 67).

In the old days the sliver was converted on a Big Wheel, and those of you lucky enough to possess one of those machines may find a new use for it here. Simply attach the sliver to the spindle and, gently rotating the wheel, allow the twist to run into the sliver.

When turning a sliver either into a top or a roving it is important to arrange the fibre so that the end that was pulled off first will be at the point where spinning will commence, so that in further attenuating the top or roving the fibre will pull out naturally, or 'flow' in the same direction as they were drawn from the comb. *Always keep in your mind's eye a stream of fibre from the sheep to the comb to the spindle, in which the direction of the fibre flow does not change.*

The Big Wheel is an ideal instrument for sliver conversion; it can be rotated slowly enough to make the twist insertion easily controllable and allows plenty of time for the operator to even out the sliver or roving if required, for if the wheel is going too fast you can just put out your hand and slow it down.

Sliver *cannot* be converted into roving on a Saxony Wheel.

I have been surprised at just how much twist can be inserted, although it does vary according to staple length and sliver density. Start off by inserting just enough twist to form a rope that will not extend, that is, the fibres will not slip past each other when, say, a 2-feet (60 cm) length is gently tugged from either end. Count carefully the number of turns of the wheel that were required to insert the amount of twist in that length of fibre, so that you can repeat the dose on the remaining sliver, and on the sliver from the other comb.

Such a roving will certainly spin comfortably. Later, with more practice and experience, you may prefer rather more twist, but start with a low twist roving first.

When the twist first runs into the roving, the fibres will still be readily extendable, and the opportunity should be taken to thin out any thick places in the sliver, should they have appeared.

Thin patches are a curse, for the twist will tend to accumulate there, causing a tightly-twisted patch with low-twist areas on either side.

If this does occur, pinch the sliver on the spindle side of the thin place and after it has been twisted, wind it on. Then lightly twist the thin patch and wind that on, then carry on with the normal density sliver that follows.

I find that direction of twist is important. It should be the opposite to that of the finished yarn. Roving 'S' for spindle 'Z', for, as we shall see later, the twist in the roving has an important part to play in the successful drafting, or thinning out, of the roving for final spinning.

Remember it is the *end* of the sliver, the last piece to be drawn off the comb, that is attached to the spindle. All you have to do is visualize the spinning wheel spindle rotating, say, clockwise, and rotate the roving spindle in the opposite direction.

Rovings are bulky articles, so if your Big Wheel has a relatively short spindle—we use 5 in (13 cm) only for cotton spinning—you will find it quite inadequate for roving production. There will not be sufficient space for any bulk of roving to be wound on, with the result that the fibres on the spindle will tend to rub and tangle with those still being twisted.

The answer is to make a longer spindle, say 10–12 in (say 25–30 cm), a truly dangerous implement to have sticking out into a room, especially if there are young children about, which is why we have the shorter spindle in position most of the time.

Perhaps it is worth observing that it is only a dangerous implement now because we are unaccustomed to meeting it in the home. In the days of the cottage industry, children would have been accustomed to seeing one in nearly every house, and treating them with the respect that they deserve, much as our children treat motor traffic today (Fig. 68).

So you don't possess a Big Wheel?

Now let me confess that, although we do possess one and do use it for roving production, more often than not it is already occupied when its use for that purpose is required, and so in desperation I one day attempted to make a roving by twisting the sliver on a hand-held spindle. To my amazement I found it to be an easy-to-control, effortless task, so I now produce 90% of my roving that way—it even has a built-in advantage!

My spindles are No. 3 knitting needles, 14 in (35·5 cm) long. In use, I hold the spindle (knitting needle) in one hand and attach the sliver to the centre by just drawing out and twisting a few fibres around it. Then, with the needle inclined almost down the length of the sliver, it is rotated between thumb and index finger—the little finger will form into a crook to hold the spindle in the hand.

After a few turns grip the spindle where the fibre is attached to it and the sliver, say, a couple of feet away from it, and gently apply some tension. If the sliver forms into a roving which is difficult to stretch, then bring the needle at right-angles to the sliver and wind the twisted length of roving on to the needle-cum-spindle.

Uneven places can easily be seen and rectified; too much twist can be removed by reversing the spindle direction, thin places can be controlled in the same manner as with the Big Wheel.

Fig. 68   'The Country School Mistress'—an engraving by P. W. Tomkins, dated 1799.

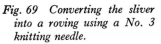
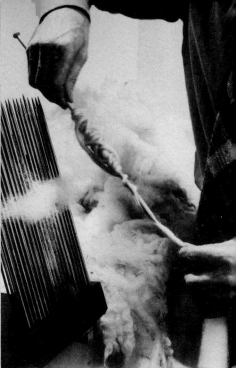

Fig. 69 Converting the sliver into a roving using a No. 3 knitting needle.

Fig. 70 A close-up of the twisting action.

To start with, insert enough twist to prevent fibre slippage under modest tension; experience will soon teach you how much is required. Take care to ensure that the twist direction is correct. Follow exactly the same rules as for the Big Wheel (Figs 69 and 70).

Now for the hidden advantage. When a roving has been made on the Big Wheel, it has to be removed from the spindle before it can be spun—it is slid off the spindle in the form of a cop.

In spinning, the roving lies in a container by the spinner's side, initially under the tension of its own weight, but towards the end this is insufficient to prevent what remains being lifted bodily towards the spinner's hand. As the diminished cop leaves the ground there is nothing to prevent the twist unwinding, and the remaining fibres can soon become an unmanageable tangled mass.

If, however, the spindle remains inside the roving, it will add weight, tension, to the roving with the result that the roving unwinds without causing a tangle. Spinning with slight tension on the roving imparts an

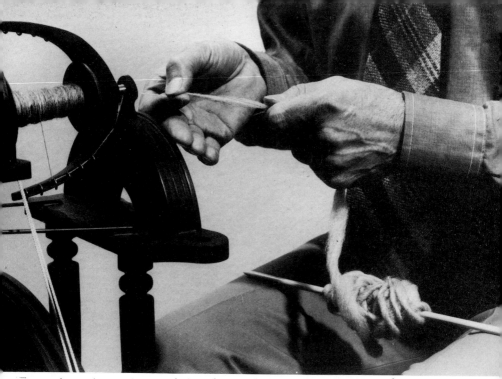

Fig. 71   The spinning position with the spindle and roving resting across the thighs—
make sure it unwinds towards your lap.

entirely different feel to it; the fibres stay more tightly coiled and are consequently more easily drawn out (drafted) in a steady, uniform quantity than when the roving is relaxed with the fibres at greater distances from each other.

You will, of course, require as many needles as the number of rovings you wish to prepare. The most I have ever sat down to spin was six, equal to about 72 feet (22 m) of roving, and at the end of that I was pleased to have the excuse for a change of work in preparing some fresh ones!

The only difficulty I have encountered in using the needles for spindles is that the fingers tend to become oily from contact with the fibre, which makes the gripping and rotation of the spindle a little difficult until the oil has been removed from both needle and hand.

To spin the roving I found it was very easy to rest the needle across my lap and spin directly from it. If the legs are separated as they are for treadling anyway, the needle ends will rest one on either thigh—trousers being perhaps slightly better than skirts. (Fig. 71.)

With the roving in your lap you can adjust the twist (usually to put more in) if necessary, and the twist will stay in all but the last 2 inches (5 cm)—just that piece of roving that will pull off the needle and hang between your hands and your lap.

Make sure that the unwinding of the roving rolls the needle *up* your lap; if it rolls towards your knees it will be forever falling on the floor!

Fig. 72 *With the end of that chapter you might feel like offering up a prayer! Spare a thought, then, for Bishop Blaize, patron saint of woolcombers, and one-time Bishop of Sebasta, Cappadocia, who, in the 2nd century suffered martyrdom by having the flesh torn off his body by iron combs.*

Chapter 5
Coloured Yarns

Colouring yarns with natural dyes can be, and is, an interesting and absorbing pastime. The combination of dyes, mordants, exhausts, etc. is limitless. There is, too, the undoubted satisfaction of having followed the process through right from the earth, as it were.

However, I think one would need to be a great expert to match a natural dye colour, made from a dye plant harvested one week, with one made from a similar plant harvested a week or two later; and the task is more difficult still if the amount of yarn needed was underestimated and a similar plant was used to dye the deficit a month or two later, when the shortfall was discovered. I agree that one should not make such mistakes, but one does.

Although natural dyes have stood the test of time in the sense that they are the oldest-known colourants used by man to stain his body, and dye his garments, he was, in a sense, making the best of a bad job—a bad job because many of the dyes were difficult to fix to fibres. They faded and they washed out.

This gave rise to a skill on the part of the textile producer in choosing dyes for his multi-coloured garments which had similar fade rates, and, as with all skills, some people were very good at it while others failed miserably. It is, furthermore, a skill often lacking today.

The treatment the fibres receive is generally very harsh in natural dye-baths, with boiling in a mordant and subsequent immersion in boiling dye liquor, hovering on the two-hour mark.

Fun though the preparation of the natural dye material can be, it is time-consuming. So, too, is the spinning of the yarn and the weaving of the material. After such an expenditure of time and labour I tend to want a product of first-class quality.

If the product contains several coloured threads, the total making a harmonious colour balance, and if, over a period of time, some colours fade or change their shade and others do not, so altering the appearance of the whole, then I have not achieved a first-class product. I have made one that is substandard; substandard because there are dyestuffs available which are more stable to light and milling—the synthetic dyes.

There is another aspect of the natural dye industry which bears some examination, and that is the growing scarcity of many of the dye plants. Most recipes require a weight-to-weight ratio, plant to material. This may not be serious for fairly common plants like weld or privet, onion or even heather, but when we come to the lichens, which are not only very small, but slow growing, then the enthusiastic dyer can soon make serious inroads into the local lichen supply. A well-organized and active guild, constantly gathering new members, can reduce dye plants in an area, especially the rarer ones, to danger level. I often ponder whether we have the authority to plunder Nature's dwindling resources so.

The spinner should be made aware that yarns made from fibres which have been dyed and then blended with undyed fibre prior to spinning are softer and more resilient, better in every way, than yarns that have been spun and then dyed.

Such fibre blending is a rarer process amongst the advocates of natural dyes than amongst the users of synthetic dyes. There are several reasons for this. One is that the traditionalists like to 'spin in the grease'—they like to spin dirty fibre. Dyeing requires scoured fleece or yarn, consequently if you wish to spin dirty fleece and want coloured yarns, you have to dye the yarn after spinning.

Another possible reason is that it is easier to free yarn from the tiny particles of dye plant that circulate in the dye bath than to keep them out of the fleece. It is often necessary to place the dye material or fleece, or both, in a muslin bag prior to vegetable dyeing for this reason. Of course, the prolonged treatment and immersion in the boiling mordant, and then dye liquor, all take their toll of the fibre qualities we desire and require; the fibres become harsh to the touch and the yarns are inclined to be frizzly.

Synthetic dyes—acid dyes for wool—because they 'take' more quickly, do not detract from the desirable qualities of the fibre to anything like the same extent, and because the colour is generally (or can be made to be) much more intense, the spinner can blend dyed with carefully measured quantities of undyed fibre until the desired shade has been achieved. Soft or pastel shades can be dyed direct, of course. But this produces a yarn of 100% dyed fibre which, although softer because of the reduced immersion time, will not be as soft as a blended yarn.

Acid dyes are relatively cheap to buy, and if price is a consideration and the business of gathering dye plants is costed to include time and transport, they are very much cheaper for a town-dweller living well away from raw material sources. I realize that this argument is a difficult one to sustain, for most of us make an outing of the dye plant gathering expedition, including it with a day in the country, a picnic and, perhaps, a visit to friends. Nonetheless, the dye so garnered is not so 'free' as it might at first sight appear to be.

I gained my knowledge of dyeing from Elsie G. Davenport's book *Your Yarn Dyeing*. In it, when talking about utensils, she mentions stainless steel containers as being a good investment in saving time in cleaning after use. It is only after trying to clean pans made of non-stainless material that you realise what an important point it is, especially when several colours are needed in a hurry. Stainless steel vessels may cost two or three times more than pans of similar size made from other metals, but it is a once-only cost, whereas the cleaning is a constantly-recurring task. We now have a stainless-steel wash boiler, with its own element and temperature control and, equally useful, a tap for emptying, which eliminates the hazard of staggering about with pans of boiling dye liquor from stove to sink. It enables us to dye 3 lb (1·4 kg) of fleece in one loading, representing a considerable saving in time. If you buy stainless steel buckets, make sure that they have a flange on the base for holding while emptying.

I do not propose to dwell at length on the subject of dyeing. There are several very good books on the subject, but the only one I have purchased was that written by Elsie Davenport.

If, when attempting to match a colour, you ensure that everything you do is an accurate repetition of your original process, then, if you use acid dyes, you can almost guarantee that the colour will be identical. You cannot hope to remember what you did, and a work book is therefore essential. Use it, write up each process fully.

You cannot work efficiently with poor or inadequate tools. An accurate balance, a true balance, is a 'must'. It is such a basic requirement for so much of our work that it is well worth purchasing one of good quality, or making one, of course.

You will also require a thermometer—a good long one registering to boiling point, a few test tubes of about 1-inch diameter, measuring cylinders, a stainless steel jug, stainless steel spoons, and stirring devices.

The only chemicals you will require for acid dye baths, apart from the dyestuff themselves, are crystalline sodium sulphate (Glauber's Salt), acetic acid 25%, formic acid, sulphuric acid and washing soda.

In assessing the process we use, one which gives us absolutely even and repeatable colours fleece after fleece, you must bear in mind that our water supply comes from a moorland stream, and that the fleeces we use come from animals which have all grazed over the same land. Whether that is important or not I do not know, but I try to stick to a sound combination, once one has been found.

When the fleece to be dyed has been brought from the store of scoured fleece, it is carefully weighed and then put to soak in a bowl of water containing 2% soda. The formula did not state whether it should be 2% of the liquid or the weight of the wool, so we chose the wool, and added 9 g ($\frac{1}{3}$ oz) of common washing soda for each 1 lb (453 g) of fibre being wetted.

We always soak the fibre in the soda solution for 1 hour, and spin it in a spin-drier to remove the surplus liquid before placing it in the dye bath. Failing a spin, I would fold the fleece in an old sheet and wring out the surplus.

Not being a chemist, I do not know how important it is that the dye should be introduced into the dye bath at a given temperature. Most dye-stuff manufacturers say 'add to a warm dye bath'—so we always add the dye when the bath reaches 40°C (104°F).

The acid dyes we use dissolve easily in a small amount of boiling water. We first of all weigh the dry wool very carefully because the saturated colours our particular process produces require 1 g of dyestuff for each 28·35 g of fibre (1 g to 1 oz, or $\frac{1}{2}$ oz of dyestuff to 1 lb of fibre).

Prior to admitting the dye we add the recommended Glauber's Salt and acetic acid, and immediately following the dye, the wetted fibre. At this point we always extract a test tube full of the liquor to act as a guide, for by dipping out a tube full of liquor every so often you will get a very good idea of how the dye is taking, by matching it against the tube of 'unused' dye liquor (Plate 3).

The fleece is turned in the vat to ensure good liquor penetration and the temperature raised to boiling. A fresh sample of liquor is extracted after 20 minutes at the boil and retained, and another at 30 minutes. It is usually a lot fainter, more dye having been taken up by the fibre. We take another at 40 minutes and if there is no change, and especially if the dye liquor is now a pale pastel shade, we turn off the heat and allow it to cool. Then, after discarding the exhausted liquor, we rinse the fleece a couple of times, spin it and hang it out to dry.

The only colour that gives us any trouble and causes us to vary the process is yellow, when we find we have to add sulphuric acid to obtain the depth of colour we require.

The point I want to make is that by following the manufacturer's instructions, making careful notes of the process and repeating the process accurately we get the same depth of colours from the same dye material year in, year out.

Coloured yarns can be made in two ways. They can be spun in plain and then dyed, or the fibres can be dyed before they are spun. For a yarn of just one colour, the difference may not be too great, although I think the yarn made from dyed fibre will tend to be more even in colour density, because, as we have already argued, the scouring of untwisted fibre is probably more thorough than that which is possible after twisting (spinning). Further, any slight variation in the dye take-up in the untwisted fibre will be evened out in the subsequent combing process—so I plump for dyed fibre every time.

However, there is another aspect of dyed fibre spinning that I find particularly interesting; the blending together of separate coloured fibres to produce yarns of quite original and outstanding hues.

Not only are the colours obtained from blended fibres very attractive, but perhaps more importantly, the quality of the yarn, relative to that which is dyed after spinning, is considerably improved by the blending process—especially if acid dyes are used.

This is because acid dyes can be made to impart a very deep, not to say brilliant, dye to the fibre. So intense are the colours that a little coloured fibre goes a very long way indeed, so that the total quantity of dyed fibre in a coloured yarn can be relatively small.

Another point in favour of acid dyes is that colour saturation is achieved in a relatively short time, somewhere between 30 to 60 minutes. This is often one-half to one-third to one-quarter of the time taken for other dyes, particularly those of the 'natural' variety. The shorter immersion in boiling liquor results in a much smaller loss of the desirable qualities of the wool fibre.

The dyed fibre, because of its intense colour, is blended with undyed until the desired shade is acquired. Sometimes only 5% of dyed fibre is used; it is rare indeed for the percentage to rise above 50.

The resultant yarn is consequently far softer, more lively, less harsh than one which has been spun first and then tortured to death first in a mordant and then in a vegetable dye bath.

It is often impossible to distinguish by feel alone the difference between an undyed yarn and one that is coloured by blending with dyed fibres.

The main problem encountered is in producing an acceptably even blend.

There are two main areas of trouble. One is associated with the fact that in sliver formation the longer fibres are more prevalent in the start of the sliver than at the end. If those long fibres happen to be the coloured elements there will be a steady bleed-off of colour from one end of the sliver to the other. Of course, it will in part be evened up when the sliver is planked, but the colour distribution may still be very uneven.

The other source of trouble occurs in the combing process.

First, then, the question of staple length for colour blending, and here we must state *that a coloured yarn from blended fibre has to be planned right from the sorting of the fleece.*

Say a material is proposed which will require a blend of 50% undyed fibre with 25% of one colour and 25% of another, total weight to be 3 lb (1,360 g). With a wastage of 10% for noils (used afterwards for woollen spinning), grot, etc. we add an extra 4¾ oz (136 g) of fibre. The important thing is that each of the three batches—the 26 oz (748 g) white (undyed) and the two batches of 13 oz (368 g) each of the coloured fibres, should not only be of the same quality, *but should all have the same staple length* (Plate 4).

If this criterion is met, there will not be any, or many, longer fibres to draw off first, and the chances of an even colour distribution in the sliver will be that much greater.

That does not mean that some areas of your fleece, the longer staple areas, for instance, must be discarded because they will not blend with the shorter fibres. They can, of course, still be used for a plain yarn, or, if more than one fleece is being used, matched with fibre of a similar staple length from other fleeces when a usable quantity has accumulated.

The method is first to work out the fibre quantity requirements and then weigh out the total amount all in fibre of as near one staple length as can be managed. This quantity has then to be sub-divided into the quantities for dyeing, dyed and dried.

It is difficult to decide on which of the two alternatives in the next stage to adopt, for you can either comb out just the quantities required for immediate spinning from the various fibre batches, or you can comb out the three batches of fibre completely, keeping each one separate, of course.

I think there is little doubt that a more even colour distribution is obtained if the dyed fibre is first rough-combed into slivers and laid aside till required, for then any slight variation in fibre length or dye take-up will be blended in, whereas, taken a few locks at a time, local variations might be more noticeable.

The disadvantage that I have found is that it is easy enough to rough-comb a vast pile of fibre, but it takes considerable extra time to blend, finish comb and spin it all up. For instance, I rough-combed 43 oz (1·2 kg) of wool in nine-and-a-half hours, or two afternoons' work over one weekend. But the blending and spinning took a further seventy-one hours, equalling ten weeks of spare-time work at weekends.

It was perhaps unfortunate that this was over January, February and March, when the ambient temperature in England is low—the time was chosen because the evenings were long—but the effect on the oil was that it stiffened up considerably. Of course, it did become freer during the combing process as the fibre mass was warmed by the combs, but it seemed to acquire a tackiness that is absent when the fibre is combed and spun the same day, as it were.

Since then I have only rough-combed a week's supply of white fibre at a time. I thought that since rarely less than 50% of the comb load would be undyed fibre, it would probably work out if all the coloured fibre was rough-combed but, say, only a week's supply of undyed fibre was combed at a time. The fresh oil in the undyed fibre would tend to merge with the staler oil in the dyed fibre and freshen things up a little. It seems to work well; the tackiness no longer occurs, and spinning is consequently that much easier.

My method is to weigh out the fibre in the required quantities, anoint with oil and water as prescribed and rough-comb (straighten). I then draw it out into a sliver, plank it, and lay the sliver on one side, paying particular attention to the maintenance of the fibre flow.

The noils are retained in a bag. Every four lots, that is, the noils from 2 combings, are themselves re-combed, and their slivers added to the sliver pile. The noils resulting from this noil combing are discarded.

We should presently end up with 3 distinct piles of sliver, one undyed, the other two of dyed fibre (Plate 5).

We have now to weigh out the sliver piles, comb-load by comb-load, in the required percentages to make the proposed final colour. If your comb holds 40 g of fibre, we shall require 20 g of white and 10 g of each of the colours. The weighing of the fibre must be exact; poor or inaccurate weighing will lead to an uneven colour blend. If yours is a true balance in which the pans are supported from underneath, their accuracy can be very much improved if you draw a mark on the vertical column under the pan which holds the fibre. Draw it level with the scale case when the pans are in balance, and you should have little difficulty in obtaining a very accurate measure if you zero to the mark for each pan load.

85

Make a note of everything you do in a work book, so you can refer to any points of detail. Particularly note percentages of colours in colour blends when you are experimenting. It is fatal to come up with a fascinating shade, and be unable to remember the magical combination which gave rise to it!

The rough-combed sliver you have weighed out will be rather thick and lumpy, and if laid side by side in a colour combination of, say, white, gold, brown, white, gold, brown, and then gathered together for lashing on, it is very likely that some pretty heavy concentrations of colour will occur.

Experience has shown that such dollops of colour are extremely difficult, in some cases impossible, to eradicate and nearly always result in an uneven colour distribution as the heavily concentrated colour—or plain—fibre is drawn off the comb—and this is the second trouble spot I mentioned.

I have found that this particular trouble can be eradicated by attenuating the slivers until they are wispy things of more or less even density, and then alternating them side by side, always taking care to keep the fibre flow in the same direction. Draw them out to about 3-foot (1 m) lengths, when 20 g of fibre will cover an area of about 6 sq. feet (0·6 sq. m), to a depth of about 1 inch (2·5 cm).

This drawing out can be a strain on your eyes. Try drawing out a sliver of white fibre against the background of a white floor and you will see what I mean .So provide yourself with a contrasting background for each of the colours you are using. A neutral grey is ideal.

Draw out some white first. Draw it out into thin, wispy, smoke-like lengths, and lay them side by side on your work bench. Don't get impatient with the job—the more cobwebby the material, the better your blend will be (Plate 6).

When about one-third of the white is layered, start on one of the colours. Treat it in the same way and lay the extended sliver evenly over the white. Follow this with another one-third of white (Plate 7), then the next colour, and finally the last of the white, and spray the mass with 6 ml of water. I find that this is particularly necessary when the sliver has been prepared some time in advance, as the water originally applied evaporates. No further oil need be applied, of course.

Now gather the mass of sliver together by rolling them into a stick of coloured candy-floss and, after placing a heated comb on the pad, start to lash on the amalgamated sliver (Plate 8).

Lash it well on to the comb, so that the fibre is caught in all the rows, not just those in front. Carry on pulling out the sliver and lashing on until the whole quantity is placed on the comb, then turn it on its side and start jigging with the second heated comb (Plate 9).

Enter the comb from the tip of the fibre mass, slowly working deeper and deeper into it, so that the amount of fibre gathered on the moving comb at each pass is relatively small.

Work the fibre from comb to comb, from hand comb to static comb, from static comb to hand comb a few times until further combing has little or no effect on the distribution of coloured fibres. No clearer guide can be given at this stage, because nearly always some coloured tufts or streaks will persist on one or other comb which no amount of combing seems to remove. Bear in mind that when the fibre is drawn off, the colour tuft will come out in a long streak, which will in any case be broken up in the planking, next lashing-on and subsequent combing (Plate 10).

So at this point, stop the combing and draw off the fibre, lay the sliver on the bench in, say, 3-foot (1 m) lengths, with the fibre flow all in one direction.

Place the noils in a bag or box marked '2', and when those from four combs have accumulated, comb them out and add the resultant sliver to the next lot of slivers from a second combing. The noils from the combed noils can be retained for carding if use of a woollen spun yarn of that colour can be made, or they may be discarded.

So far, then, we have rough-combed the bulk fibre, weighed out the quantities required for our particular colour combination and united the constituents in a second combing.

Now we will attempt to perfect the blend in a third combing. More often than not this is successfully accomplished, though occasionally a fourth combing may be required.

The third combing completes the mixing process started by the preceding operations. The heated comb is placed on the pad, and the bundle of slivers accumulated from the second combing lashed on to it in tufts of approximately 9-inch (23 cm) lengths. As before, ensure that they are held by all the rows of tines; turn the comb sideways and start jigging, again taking care to start at the fibre tips and gradually work inwards towards the tines.

It is now that the true finished colour will start to emerge. Keep on combing back and forth until the blend of fibre is even, or as even as you can get it. Then stop, and draw the fibre from the comb through the diz, and after planking, make a roving so that spinning will commence from the end that was drawn off first.

The noils from the third combing are placed in a bag marked '3', and when sufficient have accumulated are combed, and the resultant sliver placed with a pile of stage 2 combing, or if a stage 4 combing is required, with the next lot of stage 3 sliver for the final combing. You can, of course, comb out the noils, draw them off through the diz, and turn them into a roving without combining them with sliver from an earlier stage combing, but remember that the combed noils are a collection of all the short fibre, so yarn spun from such a sliver would be comparatively hairy when seen side by side with yarn in which longer fibres predominate.

The experiment is not completed until the roving has been spun and a sample piece either knitted or woven.

If you standardize your weighing and your combing, the product from a given colour combination will be a constant, and any random element it may contain will be a constant too, in the sense that it is inherent in the process.

Lovats and a whole host of other coloured yarns are an accurately repeatable possibility. The combination, or permutation, of colours is gigantic and no one lifetime would exhaust the possibilities. From a range of some 20 acid dyes for wool we use six only—crimson, yellow, brown, jade green, black and brilliant blue. A pound of dyed fibre in each of these colours will provide an area of experimenting which will produce some weeks of interesting work (Plates 11 and 12).

Weigh accurately, adopt a system of working that never varies and make a note of all the quantities you use for each experiment, and you should produce yarns of a constant quality which are quite exclusive to you. Or you may, by analysing commercial yarns under a glass, work out the percentage of the colours they contain, dye to the individual fibre shades, and make your own hand-spun copy by using the same percentages

Chapter 6
Twisting Machines
Spinning-Wheels

So far we have not mentioned the tool we are going to use to twist the fibres we have prepared into a yarn—the Spinning-Wheel.

There are two main types—the Big Wheel and the Saxony Wheel.

The Big Wheel (Fig. 73)

The Big Wheel is assumed to have evolved from the simple drop spindle in the Indian sub-continent somewhere between A.D. 500 and 1000. This is a pretty vague beginning for such an important machine. Starting life as a 'charkha', its use gradually spread westwards, until around 1300 it first appeared in the British Isles.

By then the wheel size had increased and its base was raised from the ground on legs, enabling the spinner to sit on a chair to operate it. Later its wheel size was increased again and the spinner stood up while she worked.

Fig. 73 A simple Big Wheel. It gathered a variety of names. The English called it simply a 'Big Wheel', the Welsh called it the 'Welsh Wheel', the Scots the 'Muckle Wheel', modern technologists call it the 'One Thread Wheel'. It is also called the 'Jersey Wheel', the 'High Wheel', the 'Walking Wheel', the 'Great Wheel' and the 'Long Wheel' (Ireland).

Its claim to fame is that, after its introduction, for the first time the amount of twist inserted in a given length of yarn could be repeated accurately, which must have led to a dramatic improvement in yarn quality. It also produced yarn much faster than the drop spindle.

It will spin just about any animal fibre and short staple vegetable fibre. It was the Big Wheels, turning in cottages throughout the textile areas, that helped to lay the foundations of the British textile industry. It inspired James Hargreaves to make his Jenny, which gave such impetus to the Industrial Revolution, and centuries before that, it sent the Sleeping Beauty into a coma for forty years! With all that behind it, what's in a name!

The Big Wheel is easy to use, and will produce a worsted thread effortlessly.

Its main drawbacks are the amount of space it occupies, and the difficulty experienced in plying or cabling yarns.

The Big Wheel is a logical extension of the drop spindle idea. Instead of the spindle being supported by the thread it twists, it is turned on its side, supported between bearings, and the whorl, which now becomes a pulley, is driven by a band which passes around the big wheel.

If the wheel is rotated, the pulley and the spindle will also rotate, the amount of rotation being dependent upon the relative diameters of the pulley and the wheel.

If a length of yarn is attached to the spindle about halfway down its length and held at 45 degree to it, the spindle rotation will cause the yarn to spiral up the spindle until it reaches the point, where it will slip off. It slips off at each successive turn of the spindle; each time it slips off one turn of twist has been inserted in the length of yarn—it is as simple as that! (Fig. 74).

Fig. 74 Close-up of spindle tip.

Fresh fibre attached to the end of the yarn into which the twist is allowed to run will be twisted into a yarn, the diameter of which will be controlled by the amount of fibre the spinner allows to be caught up in the twist. As the fibres are caught the fibre mass is drawn steadily away from the spindle, which is rotating just enough to insert sufficient twist to form the fresh fibres into a yarn.

The process works particularly well with short or very short fibres— which gave it yet another name—the Short Fibre Wheel. Cottons and short staple animal fibre can be twisted and drafted in a continuous movement of the hand holding the fibre away from the spindle as it rotates, the other hand meanwhile rotating the wheel. If the revolutions are counted and the length of yarn made at each draw is identical, a uniform length of yarn will result.

Very short fibre wheels were, and still are, made with quite a small diameter and high spindle ratio, 25:1 to 40:1 being the norm; short fibres generally require considerable twist to form them into a yarn of reasonable strength.

Longer staple fibres may require less twist, but because of the increased fibre length, the influence of the twist extends further into the fibre supply (the fibres held in the hand) and tends to twist them to such an extent that separation (drafting) becomes extremely difficult. Two-handed drafting then became necessary. Wheels of small diameter quickly stop rotating if allowed to free-wheel, and so the diameter of the wheel was increased to give it more mass. It would then free-wheel for several revolutions after receiving one flick of the spinner's hand, allowing two-handed drafting, and the production of worsted yarns, among others.

It is an interesting sidelight on the subject that in my researches I have come across several references in textbooks which say that worsted yarns, because they required two-handed drafting, could not be spun on the Big Wheel, that they were spun on the drop spindle and later on the Saxony Wheel.

My own experience does not substantiate this at all. I learnt my worsted spinning on a Big Wheel and found it an easy task not only to perform the drafting but to exercise a very accurate control on the twist. I do not believe the practical hand-spinners ever experienced any difficulty in producing a worsted thread on them either, neither do I believe that the much more expensive Saxony Wheel ever reached the pre-Hargreaves cottage industry. *An inventory dated 1575 gave the value of a spinning wheel and stool as 8d. Since the Saxony Wheel had only been in use on the Continent for 75 years, this account is rather unlikely to have referred to one of them.*

John James, in his *History of the Worsted Manufacture in England*, published in 1857, would seem to bear this out, for he states on page 335:

'. . . but in the worsted business there is a peculiarity in the yarn spun by this wheel which gives it a great advantage over mill spun yarns, namely, the thread was spun from the middle portion of the sliver, thus drawing the wool out even and fine. The best spinners would, on this wheel, spin fine qualities of wool to as high a count as 50s.'

(As we shall see later, 50s worsted = 560 yards $\times$ 50 = 28,000 yards per lb of yarn, equal to 16 miles!)

It is, however, only fair to point out that, reading James after many years as a practical wool comber and worsted spinner, it is obvious that his sources of information were not always reliable when it came to practical, as opposed to historical, fact.

When a length of yarn has been made—how long will depend on the spinner's stature and ability—the fibre supply is stopped and the wheel is turned a set number of times to insert the additional twist necessary to give the yarn the strength required for its prescribed end use.

The spindle direction is then reversed ('backed off' was the trade term) to unwind the yarn that had spiralled up the spindle point. The hand holding the fibre and yarn is now moved across towards the wheel so that the yearn is at 90 degrees to the spindle. This is again rotated in the direction used for spinning (twisting). This winds the yarn on to the spindle to form a cop. Towards the end of the wind-on, with about 18 inches (almost 0·5 m) of yarn left, the hand with the fibre is again moved to the 45 degrees position, the yarn spirals up the spindle again, and spinning (twisting) recommences (Fig. 75).

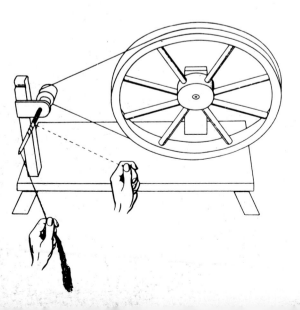

Fig. 75   The hand in the position it would assume at the commencement of the drafting action. The wheel is rotated slowly as the hand is drawn away 3, 4 or even 5 ft (1, 1·2 or 1·5 m). Drafting ceases. The wheel is rotated to give the required amount of twist to the yarn. The wheel is then backed off, the hand moved across until the yarn is at right-angles to the spindle, and the yarn wound on, returning to the drafting position again when about 18 in (46 cm) of yarn remains between the spindle and the hand.

1   The fibre on the left has been scoured; that on the right is 'in the grease'.

2   The instant effect of immersing 8oz (227g) of dirty fleece in a sink full of scouring agent – the lather vanishes like ice in the Sahara.

3 Assessing the dye take-up — the tube of liquor on the right was extracted 20 minutes before that on the left. This illustration shows the stainless steel wash-boiler in which all our fibre is dyed.

4   The batches of fibre for colour blending must all be of as nearly the same staple length as possible.

5   The woolcomber's bench, planked sliver, yellow, brown and white.

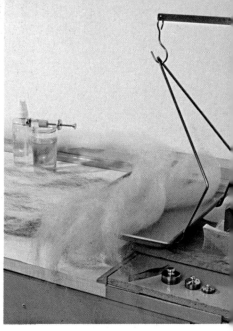

6 Draw out the sliver into fine cobwebs of
   colour, and layer them, alternating the
   colour as you go.

7 One-third white, followed by the brow
   and another one-third white. The 1c
   yellow has just been weighed.

8 The planked sliver, layered and ready to
   be rolled.

9 The heated comb, loaded with 40g
   coloured fibre, 20g white, 10g yello
   10g brown.

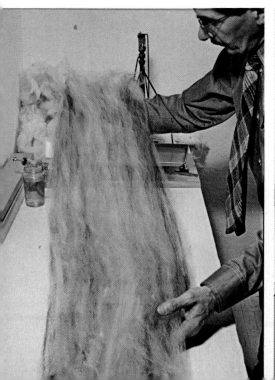

10   Sometimes a coloured streak persists, which no amount of combing will remove. Compare
      fibre with Plate 9.

11   From a range of 20 acid dyes, we use only 6 – Brown, Jade Green, Crimson, Blue, Yellow
      and Black.

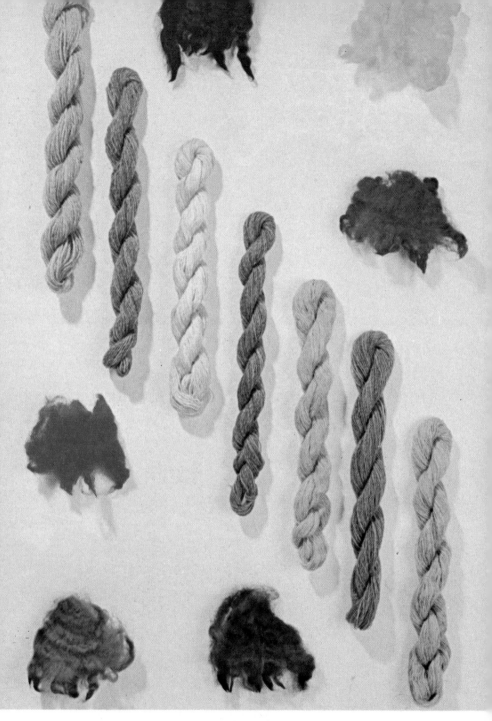

12   Left to Right. *Hanks of yarn composed of: 35g White (undyed), 5g Black; 35g White
      (undyed), 3g Red, 2g Brown; 35g White (undyed), 5g Green; 35g White (undyed),
      5g Blue; 35g White (undyed), 5g Red; 20g White (undyed), 10g Brown, 10g Yellow;
      35g White (undyed), 5g Brown.*

13 A cardigan made from hand-knitted, hand-spun worsted yarn made from blending 50%
undyed with 25% Yellow and 25% Brown. Total weight 2lb (907g), a minimum
of 23 separate blendings and combings.

14   *Spinning a roving of the same colour against a background of the cardigan, blended a year previously.*

The process, then, is intermittent, being low twist draft (draft = feeding the fibre to the twisted yarn), twist insertion, backing off, winding on, low twist draft, etc.

The Big Wheel is a useful and accurate tool because once the number of revolutions the spindle makes to the wheel is known, the same amount of twist can be inserted in a yarn of given length, and repeated and repeated and repeated. The length might be from the spindle tip to the wheel axle, sometimes made exactly a yard apart, or could be anything the spinner desired, from spindle to door post or a broom handle propped up in a bucket, but most, I have no doubt, judged it by eye and reach alone. Similarly, with the revolutions, you could have a rag tied to one of the spokes to catch your eye as it rotated, or something on the rim that clicked against the stand at each revolution; anything to help you count the amount of twist that was going in the yarn—but again my guess is that more often than not it was counted by use alone.

Very short fibres like cotton can be spun easily by turning the wheel with one hand and drawing out (drafting) the fibres with the other. Longer fibres, combing quality wool for instance, would certainly need two hands for drafting. It is then that the larger diameter and weight of the Big Wheel is an advantage, for it will continue to rotate for some time with one flick of the wrist, allowing two-handed drafting to continue.

Big Wheels were often crude machines—they wobbled, they grunted and they groaned, they squeaked . . . but they worked! No specialist wheel-maker was required; any local woodworker could knock one up, consequently they were found in just about every cottage in the textile producing areas, and they remained the main source of cotton, woollen and worsted yarns right up until the invention of the Jennies, Water Frames and Mules (Fig. 76).

Fig. 76 Spinning with the Great Wheel.

Then, because they had little or no value as a tool, and no intrinsic value, I think that they were probably converted into firewood. Certainly, considering the vast numbers that were in use, very few indeed of this type of spinning-wheel have survived.

It is an interesting sidelight that the tellers of fairy stories got it right. The fairy tale Sleeping Beauty *did* prick her finger on the spindle of her spinning-wheel—her Big Wheel. It was the Victorian illustrators who got it wrong, who drew the only wheel known to them—the Saxony Wheel, upon which there is no sharp point—so some writers decided that it must have been the distaff that caused the wound. Both writers and illustrators should have known that all the fairies had fled long before 1480, which is when the first known illustration of the Saxony Wheel principle was published.

I think it is reasonable to conclude that the Big Wheel development was logical, that sooner or later it was bound to happen, but that it took some 4,000 years of drop spindle usage is an indication that survival comes first and that man needs some slight security before he is able to sit and think.

The Saxony Wheel (Fig. 77)

Roughly 1,000 years later, think he did, because the Saxony principle is the product of an intellectual genius—or it might have been more than one—we just do not know. All we do know for certain is that the first known illustration of the principle is in the *Waldburg Hausbuch*, printed

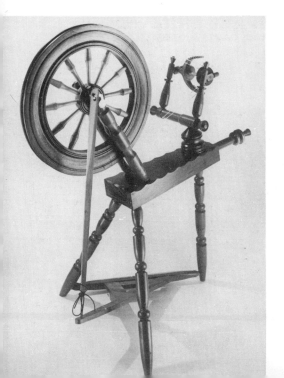

Fig. 77 The Horizontal Saxony Wheel.

in 1480, and that Leonardo da Vinci's sketch book of 1495 shows a much more advanced design. The *Glockendon Miscal*, 1524, shows a wheel being driven by a treadle, but who invented these things, or who assembled the various inventions into the Saxony spinning wheel, we have no idea at all.

The big advance made by the Saxony Wheel was that it enabled the spinner to make a yarn and wind it on in one unbroken, continuous process.

No more draft, twist, back off, wind on. But drafting, twisting, and winding on taking place simultaneously.

Let us take a look at the twisting method first. With the Big Wheel and simple spindle, you will recall that one end of the yarn was fixed to the spindle, and so, as the spindle rotated, the yarn attached to it had to rotate also. Twist was then bound to run up the length of yarn into the fibre supply.

With the Saxony Wheel the yarn is not attached to the spindle at all. Twisting is made possible by making the spinning end of the spindle hollow—it has a hole bored down it, connecting with another hole bored through the spindle at right-angles to it, so that the yarn passes down the inside of the spindle and emerges through one or other of the two outlets made by the hole bored across the spindle.

You can see that if a length of yarn is passed into the hollow end of the spindle and pulled out of one or other of the two outlets, and then the spindle rotated, the yarn must rotate with the spindle and twist will be inserted in the yarn (Fig. 78).

Fig. 78 Yarn passing into the hollow spindle end emerges through a hole bored at right angles through the spindle. Thus the yarn, although not attached to the spindle, has to rotate with it.

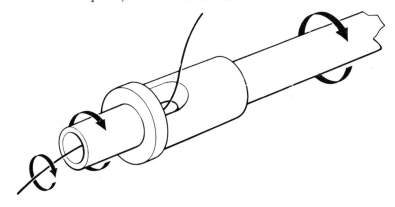

The spindle is driven, as before, by a belt from the wheel driving a pulley—called the 'spindle whorl'—fixed to one end of it by, in the better machines, a left-hand thread, so that it cannot undo in use.

Because the spinning end of the spindle is hollow, the bearings can now be placed at either end of the spindle, the yarn going through the bearing inside the spindle, as it were.

It is obvious that the yarn we have twisted cannot be made to wind on the spindle, since both it and the yarn are rotating in unison. So a bobbin was made to fit on the spindle, between the spindle eye and the whorl, with a groove at one end of it so that it could be rotated by a second belt from the wheel.

If the bobbin pulley is smaller in diameter than that of the spindle whorl, the bobbin will rotate faster and the yarn will be wound on as it is being twisted. In point of fact, one band looped around the wheel twice was used to drive the unit, one loop going over the bobbin, the other over the whorl.

It now only requires some means of transporting the yarn from the spindle eye on to the bobbin in such a way that it can be distributed evenly over its surface.

A horse-shoe-shaped piece of wood called a 'flyer' does the task admirably; there are two arms on the horseshoe for balance and the yarn is carried up along them on a series of hooks, or hecks. These are spaced at intermediate distances on each arm so that by changing from one arm to the other in spinning, an even build-up of yarn over the surface of the bobbin is possible (Fig. 79).

That is the basic principle of the Saxony spinning-wheel.

Fig. 79 *The rotation of the spindle will twist the yarn, which is drawn through the hollow spindle tip up over the arm of the flyer and, because the bobbin rotates faster than the spindle, wound on to the bobbin core.*

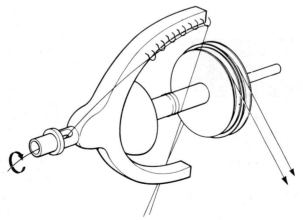

There are many niceties that we shall have to consider as we go along, but one thing all Saxony Wheels have in common is the hollow spindle to which is fixed a flyer, between the arms of which rotates a bobbin. Both bobbin and spindle are rotated by one band looped twice around a drive wheel which is usually treadle-operated.

Saxony spinning-wheels fall into two main design categories: vertical and horizontal, so called because on one the spinning mechanism is located above the wheel, whilst in the other it is to one side of it (Figs 80 and 77).

Horizontal wheels are mainly anything but! The platform supporting the wheel and spinning unit usually slopes towards the spinner's right. There is, though, a sort of sub-division of very delicate flax or cotton spinning-wheels which are truly horizontal, mounted on either a cabinet stand or made for resting on a table.

Fig. 80   A delicate Vertical Wheel on which the spindle is positioned at about 65°.

Fig. 81   A more robust Vertical Wheel with the spindle dead centre to the top of the wheel.

Selecting a Wheel

My own conclusions about spinning-wheels are based on engineering principles and experience.

Power is supplied to the machine by a treadle. It is the wheel that transmits the energy imparted by the treadle to the spindle and lifts the treadle again for the next power stroke downwards. There are no hard-and-fast rules in spinning-wheel design; there are some wheels, for instance, which are made to give a power stroke both up and down, but they are somewhat rare.

The wheel is nothing more than a flywheel; if it is heavy enough it will make your work child's play, but if too light, then treadling will become work indeed.

A flywheel needs mass, weight—the thicker, the heavier the rim the better. It is worth noting, I think, that wheels that were made in the days when they were being used for earning a living were made from hard, dense timber, and had good solid rims. The thin-rimmed Scandinavian wheels, whose design was dictated by their softer, lighter timber, are of much more recent origin. It is true that a wheel of larger diameter can have a thinner rim equal to the same mass as a smaller, thicker rim, but there are very real practical disadvantages to a rim of too great a diameter, which we will discuss in a minute.

Power is transmitted to the wheel via the treadle and crank. The throw of the crank will determine the amount of upward and downward movement of the spinner's foot. Cranks vary from about a $2\frac{1}{2}$- to 1-inch throw (6·3–2·5 cm), giving a total foot movement of from 5 to 2 inches (12·7–5 cm). Just imagine the fatigue of flapping your foot up and down 5 inches for hours on end, and you will see it is a matter which bears consideration. A 3-inch (about 8 cm) travel is comfortable for most people but 4 inches (10 cm) is as much as I would tolerate and would be ample for a very heavy flywheel indeed. Before buying a wheel I would certainly want to sit and treadle it to see if the foot movement was within my comfort range. That is important because it is impossible to alter.

But perhaps the most important consideration is the type of yarn you want to make on your machine. The factors which control the yarn type are:

1   the type and length of fibre, whether animal or vegetable, whether long staple combing quality wools or long flax fibres or short wool fibres, or shorter still cotton fibres;

2   the amount of fibre present in the yarn, determining its diameter;

3 the amount of twist required in the yarn, which largely governs its strength.

Since it is for twist insertion that the spinning-wheel was made, it is somewhat surprising that this aspect of hand-spinning has received so little attention from both teachers and students alike. On many occasions I have asked anyone amongst audiences at spinning meetings to raise their hands if they know the number of revolutions the spindle of their spinning machines make to one of the drive wheel. It is beyond belief that they could all have been shy, so one can only conclude that no-one knew—and I have asked that question many times.

Yet such knowledge is fundamental to yarn production.

If we take some wool fibres, hold one end and start to twist the other, the action of the twist will force the fibres together. Surprisingly little twist will do this, producing a soft, springy yarn ideal for knitted fabrics or weft for bulk filling. More twist will force the fibres closer together, making a hard, thready yarn with reduced elasticity and spring but proportionally increased strength—a yarn suitable for a warp thread. More twist still may produce a hard yarn which snarls up the moment that end-to-end tension is relaxed. Such a yarn is principally used for special effects, plied with a soft spun yarn to produce a curl or loop yarn.

Further twisting may cause individual strands of fibre to rupture and so weaken the thread.

The amount of twist inserted in a yarn will depend not only on the proposed end use but upon the length (staple) of the fibres being twisted, and the amount of fibre being twisted, which will, of course, govern the size or diameter of the resultant yarn.

Perhaps it will help if, without being too precise, we say that a reasonably fine yarn for a single knitting wool, spun from a 5-inch staple combed sliver for a soft christening shawl, might require 4 twists per inch (TPI). The same quantity of fibre spun into a similar yarn for making into a two-ply knitting wool yarn for a cardigan, might require 7 TPI, since some of the twist would be unwound in the plying process. (See Chapter 10.)

An insertion of 6 TPI in the same fibre quantity might produce a medium singles yarn for weft, whilst a warp might require 10 TPI.

Jumping the gun a little, it is perhaps worth explaining here that the accurate spinster feeds the machine with a stated quantity of fibre at each turn of the wheel; to make the wheel go round she has to press down once with her foot on the treadle. If the wheel rotates the spindle six times for each time it turns—a 6:1 ratio—then a yarn of 6TPI will be produced if the spindle is fed with 1 inch (2·5 cm) of fibre every time the spinster's foot presses the treadle. If the spindle rotates 12 times for every once of the wheel, then you have to feed it with 2 inches (5 cm) of fibre every time the treadle is pressed, if a 6 TPI yarn is required. It is as simple as that, *but you must know what you are doing, and why.*

It is useless to expect spinning to be an unhurried pleasure if you attempt to spin a soft yarn for a baby's robe requiring, say, 4 TPI on a spinning wheel with a 20:1 wheel-to-spindle ratio. This will require 5 inches of fibre fed to it for each wheel revolution, for each pump of the treadle; to do that accurately and effortlessly is a near impossibility.

Most spinners specialize in yarns of one quality; a great number spin all their weft, for instance, buying their warps from commercial spinners. Others may spin only for knitting. So it is important that the spinning-wheel purchased should spin most easily those yarns the spinner produces in the greatest quantity.

I have only ever seen one spinning-wheel with a range of pulleys that enabled it to be converted readily to spin cotton 22 TPI, worsted warp 10 TPI, worsted weft 7 TPI, plied knitting yarns 6 TPI and singles knitting yarn 4 TPI—and I made that myself.

So count the revolutions the flyer does to that of the wheel, to make certain the wheel will produce the yarn you want it to, in a manner which is within your capabilities to control. The spindle orifice should be large enough to accommodate the largest yarn you are ever likely to spin. A small orifice will be very restricting (Figs 82, 83 and 84).

Fig. 84 Maid-of-all-Work. The ½-in (12·7 mm) orifice will accept the largest of yarns yet still spin the most delicate required — the small orifice can only spin fine yarns.

Fig. 82 These three spindles (Figs 82-84) are all accepting the same piece of yarn. A very small orifice on a medium sized wheel for flax.

Fig. 83 Medium orifice ¼-in (6·3 mm) diameter.

Another important point is that the wind-on should be extremely rapid. We will go into the reasons later, but it is easy to see whether or not a wheel is suitable in this respect, for there should be a truly massive difference in the diameter of the spindle and bobbin whorls. The spindle whorl should be the larger, always. If the drive bands are like Fig. 85 (left), avoid it like the plague, but if they are like Fig. 85 (right), then you need have little worry (Figs 86 and 87).

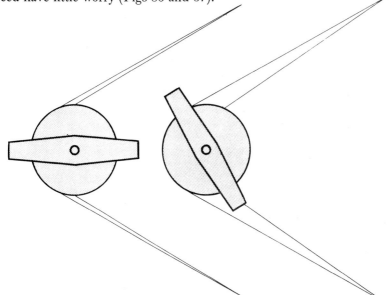

Fig. 85   Left   *Drive band loops close together indicate small difference between bobbin and spindle whorl diameter, causing a slow wind-on.*
       Right   *A better ratio between the two, with the likelihood of more evenly twisted yarn.*

Fig. 86 Shadowgram of a poorly-designed spinning unit; not only would it produce overtwisted yarns with an empty bobbin, but the two diameters on the spindle whorl are so nearly identical as to be pointless.

Fig. 87 Shadowgram showing more suitable proportion, giving a rapid wind-on which could be maintained constant from empty to full bobbin core.

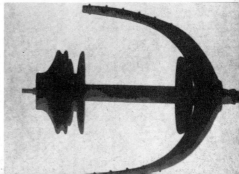

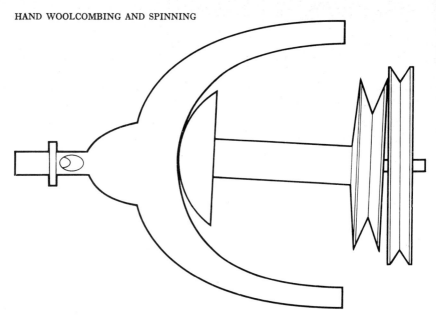

Fig. 88   Wear in bobbin bearing, causing bobbin and spindle whorl to jam together, reducing wind-on to near zero. Increasing belt tension only aggravates the problem.

Regard with caution any wheel with the spinning-unit fitted closely to the wheel, for this can so reduce the arc of contact of the drive band that higher than normal belt tensions have to be used, making the effort required more tiring.

I must admit that I have only come across a couple of instances of it, but someone had bought those wheels in good faith and it is a very difficult fault to cure.

Always check for wear in the bobbin bearings, and avoid any wheel where these bearings are just plain wood. You see, all the pressure, tension, drive-force, call it what you will, comes on the bobbin drive pulley, which is situated at the extreme end of the bobbin, so the wear is not evenly distributed between the two bearings but concentrated on the one nearest the spindle whorl.

The effect of wear on that bearing is that the bobbin gradually develops a list relative to the spindle (Fig. 88). When the list becomes excessive the bobbin starts to bind against the spindle whorl, and ceases to rotate independently. Wind-on becomes slow or may cease altogether, resulting in a harsh over-spun yarn.

102

Fig. 89   Close-up of end of bobbin, nylon bush, shim material, and metal bearing sleeve cut from it.

The spinster's usual reaction, believing the trouble to be caused by the belt slipping, is to increase the tension, to increase the wind-on, but in this case it only makes matters worse. She tries another bobbin, which may not be so badly worn, or being empty, will not require so much tension and may still work reasonably well. And so we have yet another 'temperamental' spinning-wheel.

The answer is to fit bobbin bearings that simply will not wear out. If you have the equipment, bore out the bobbins and fit nylon bushes. Failing that, a quite satisfactory job can be made from a shim of metal cut and bent around the spindle and then pushed inside the worn bobbin bearing. Cut a paper pattern first to enable you to cut the metal accurately to size (Fig. 89). It is essential that the bobbin rotates freely under all conditions of spinning.

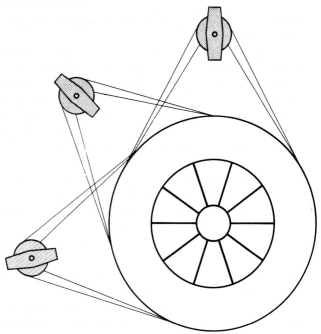

*Fig. 90   The same effort will be required to drive the spinning unit regardless of
its position relative to the wheel.*

So now we come to the controversy of vertical or horizontal. I am always
being told that vertical wheels are more difficult to use, more tiring, do not
spin well . . . and so on. It really is a load of rubbish and it is high time
people started to use a spot of reason in this argument.

If you make two spinning-wheels identically, and two identical spinning-
units, the same amount of effort will be required to operate them regardless
of their relative positions (Fig. 90).

It is true that some vertical wheels were made in a much more delicate
fashion than was common with horizontal wheels. They were lighter, often
smaller; some were made for flax, some for cotton, and would no doubt be
difficult to use on fibres other than those for which they were designed.

A vertical wheel of sensible proportions is every bit as easy to use as a
horizontal wheel of similar size and has the added advantage today that it
takes up considerably less floor space.

How does a prejudice start? Well, I would suggest that this one started
in your cradle, or very near to it. For we must all admit that when we first

saw a vertical wheel, it just did not look right—not like a spinning-wheel *ought* to look.

I once carried a notebook about with me and I asked people with whom I came into conversation to draw me an outline of a spinning-wheel, offering them a clean page each time so that no-one could see what had been drawn before. I asked school-teachers, bank managers, our Member of Parliament, doctor, garage attendant, laundry driver, accountant, vet., civil servant, grocer—and so on—women and men, fifty in all, and without a single exception they drew the horizontal wheel, which from childhood fairy tales they had remembered as a spinning-wheel.

Such conditioning must be very difficult to overcome. We naturally want our first spinning-wheel to conform to our ideas of what a spinning-wheel ought to be. We want our friends to recognize it for what it is . . . and so the horizontal wheel goes on going on!

In the Belfast Museum collection in Northern Ireland there are—or were when I was there—20 horizontal and 18 vertical wheels, so there was no deep-seated prejudice against vertical wheels in the days when wheels were used as a means of livelihood.

I have often wondered why so many more Saxony Wheels have survived than Big Wheels, for we know that in terms of numbers made and in use, the Big Wheel far exceeded all others. It is likely that the more complicated Saxony wheel was considerably more expensive and, except in the flax-spinning areas, never reached the cottage industry in any great numbers. When it did it must have been a relatively valuable implement, more likely to be retained after its usefulness had departed that the clumsy, valueless Big Wheel.

Quite when it became a symbol of good housewifeliness to be 'good at her wheel' I do not know, but by the 19th century people who had never done a stroke of work in their lives were depicted at their wheels. Queen Victoria was even photographed at her wheel—a horizontal one, of course (Fig. 91).

Today I would be very chary indeed about buying a spinning-wheel from an antique dealer. So often those offered are mixtures of wheels which have been acquired at various times and assembled to give the general appearance of a working wheel.

I have yet to see any spinning-wheel maker specify the spindle-to-wheel ratio of his product, or state that he will make it to suit the yarns the spinner requires. Spinning-wheels are sold as spinning-wheels and nothing more. You just have to hope that you can adapt your requirements to the one you buy.

Fig. 91   Queen Victoria
'As a Spinner'.

The following chapter will at least give you a working knowledge of your subject, so that you can better assess the wheels you are offered.

Before we leave this topic we had better mention the various parts of the wheel. The piece upon which the machine is assembled is called the 'table', 'platform', or 'base'. The two sticks supporting the wheel are the wheel columns or 'bearers'; the wheel has a rim, hub and spokes. The axle and crank are most commonly permanently fixed to the hub. The two pieces which house the spindle bearings are most commonly called the 'maidens', sometimes the 'sisters'. (Fig. 92.)

One of the maidens, and sometimes both, is made so that it can twist in its socket or be removed completely from the mother-of-all. This is to facilitate the withdrawal of the spindle for bobbin replacement; but the very fact of their freedom to move provides a possible hazard in that they can also get out of alignment and impose considerable drag on the spindle.

It is perhaps worth mentioning that the spindle should be able to rotate very freely indeed. I disagree strongly with people who advocate using the maidens as a brake to retard spindle rotation in an endeavour to increase the relative speed of the bobbin. The better way to do that is to deepen the groove in the bobbin whorl. Retarding the spindle makes the energy required to operate the machine that much greater.

The spindle pulley is often called a 'whorl' or 'wharfe'. The spindle, bobbin and flyer are collectively known as the spinning-unit. The maidens are housed in the mother-of-all, which in turn is an integral part of the tensioning device. The piece of wood which joins the treadle to the crank is the connecting rod, con-rod, 'pitman' or 'footman'.

In use, your wheel will require lubrication at wheel axle, crank pin, treadle bearings, spindle bearings and bobbin bearings. 'Three-in-One' oil is sold in small cans and is handy to have around, but any engine oil will do. An excess of oil will stain the wood, but I would rather that than too little, causing a hard-to-work, squeaky, rattly machine, constantly crying for the attention its insensitive owner fails to give. There are now some dry lubricants obtainable in powder form, which seem to work very well and do not stain the timber.

Fig. 92 Parts of the Saxony spinning-wheel.

Never house your wheel in a centrally-heated room unless the ambient humidity is at least equal to that outdoors, but I would say *never* place your wheel in a centrally-heated area. It can cause untold havoc; it dries the timber right out, causing it to shrink however well it has been seasoned. Joints become loose all over the machine, and it may soon deteriorate to a rickety, wobbly shadow of its former glory.

The drive band is a continuous length of cord looped twice round the wheel, one loop going over the spindle whorl, one over the bobbin pulley. It is obvious, then, that at some point or other the loops must cross.

It is rather important that the cross should occur in a way that allows the band going to the smaller diameter bobbin pulley to be inside that for the larger diameter spindle whorl, then the loops will not foul each other.

It is easy enough to thread the band material around the wheel and spindle unit and observe where and how the cross occurs. Ideally, it should occur between the wheel and spindle on the delivery side.

A lot of instruction has been written about drive bands. My own thoughts are these. The work of the drive band is two fold; it has to drive the spindle .and at the same time allow the bobbin to slip or be static relative to the spindle. A band of too great a cross-section may drive the unit well but may make slippage difficult except at very low tension, while a mono-filament material may slip well but make spinning difficult because it allows the spindle to slip as well, except at high tension.

Picture cord is a happy compromise, so too is bricklayer's line cord—all you have to do is join it. Do you splice it? *Can* you splice it? Or sew it? One thing is certain—you cannot knot it or the knot may catch in the cross or jam in the narrow grooves of the two wharves. So splicing or sewing is the answer. Set the tension about half-way between the total movement available and pass the band material around the wheel and pulleys, pull the ends together, allow half an inch (say 2 cm) for joining, and cut across the two. Then sew or splice. With the tension at half way, this should allow adjustment to counter either shrinkage or stretch, and allow you to slacken off completely for bobbin removal. Bands do shrink or stretch alarmingly, and then the tedious job of splicing or sewing has to start all over again.

In 1961, a friend of mine told me he was using nylon cord on the overhead drive of his lathe. Easy to join, he said; just heat the ends and press the molten blobs together, then roll them between finger and thumb. I tried it; it worked. From lathe to spinning-wheel was a short jump, and I have used it ever since. The joint is strong; I have never had one part. It is small, so does not catch in anything, and is made in a minute. A match will do, though its soot will make a black blob of the join. You will find a methylated spirit flame much cleaner.

Nylon cord is obtainable in several sizes and surface textures. Traditionalists do not like it for some reason, but they will cheerfully use machine-made string, which is just as incongruous if they only stop to think about it.

Chapter 7
Worsted Spinning

We have said earlier that the spinning process involves treadling the machinery with one foot, whilst presenting a precise quantity of fibre to the spinning unit with both hands, the brain synchronizing these movements so that their product is uniform.

Bear in mind that what you are about to acquire is a knack, moreover it is an extremely simple one, a relatively low order of skill, one that we should be ashamed of not being able to acquire rather than exultant at having done so.

Admittedly, it is a bit like rubbing your tummy and patting your head at the same time, and you can acquire that knack easily enough if you practise one of the movements first until you can do it effortlessly, then practise the other, and finally combine the two. So we, with our spinning, will start with one movement first—that of treadling.

You will, of course, by now have assembled your wheel, have placed the drive band over the respective whorls, and twiddled the knob which controls the tension. So, before we do anything else, adjust the tension so that the bobbin and flyer are just being driven when the wheel is rotated by hand.

It is, I think, very important that you should find a comfortable chair, one that brings your hands to a convenient height to reach spindle, flyer and wheel without excessive body movement.

Just any old chair will not do. You are going to occupy it for long periods of time; you want to be able to get out of it reluctantly, not with the feeling of 'Thank heavens *that's* over' as you ease the pain where the sharp edge of the chair has been cutting into the backs of your thighs.

I have no idea how the low spinning stools ever came to be so named, unless they were used by spinsters who sat at their Big Wheels, but even then I should think they were far from comfortable. I certainly could never use one—sitting with my knees knocking my elbows and my tummy doubled up would soon make spinning purgatory. So, to coin a phrase— if you're sitting comfortably, then I'll begin.

Rest one foot on the treadle. It doesn't really matter which one; I have only ever seen one left-footed treadler, but she was a jolly good spinster. So use the foot which comes naturally.

Turn the wheel by hand to ensure that the crank is at the bottom of the stroke. Is the platform level? Or is it tilting upwards? Worse still, is it tilting downwards?

Let us start by adjusting the string or leather which attaches the treadle platform to the con-rod; tie them so that the platform is level. Now, with your foot on the platform, turn the wheel until the crank is at the top of its stroke. Is your foot now at a too acute angle? I am sorry for you if it is, for it probably means that the crank throw is excessive. If the angle is too great for comfort, you can even things out a little by allowing the platform to fall slightly below being level at the bottom of the throw; but so much movement will always be rather productive of aches, and will tend to limit the time you can, with comfort, work your machine. Happily, such wheels are rare.

If, when the crank is at the top of its throw, you feel you could have the platform at a greater angle, then that is all to the good, for it will mean that the platform is tilted slightly upwards when at the bottom of the stroke, and that is a comfortable position at rest. So shorten the thongs, say, $\frac{1}{2}$ inch (1·3 cm) and re-test the foot position. If all is now quite comfortable, we can start the machine going.

It must be obvious that with the crank at top dead centre (TDC) or bottom dead centre (BDC), all the weight in the world applied to the treadle will not make the wheels go round, and that the ideal starting position for the crank is either at 10 o'clock or at 2 o'clock as you sit looking at it; 10 o'clock for starting the wheel rotating in an anti-clockwise direction, 2 o'clock for a clockwise direction.

So, with your foot on the treadle, turn the wheel until the crank is at 2 o'clock. Remove your hand from the wheel and press down with the foot, trying to take the pressure off when the platform is at the bottom of the stroke and allowing the foot to be lifted with the momentum you imparted to the wheel by pressing down. After all, that is its job—it is nothing more than a flywheel to enable you to convert an intermittent, reciprocal movement into a continuous rotative one which will drive your twisting apparatus with a near-constant speed in a continuous direction.

Allow the wheel to carry the crank over TDC and, as the platform starts to fall, press down with the foot again. Treadling is the knack of sensing when to apply the pressure and when to allow your foot to idle. But be gentle—you are using a machine which is far from robust, so apply your power in moderation. At first the crank may not even go high enough to carry over TDC; in desperation you give a frantic press on the treadle . . . and the wheel spins gaily backwards! It might even go over TDC and you find yourself treadling merrily, but in the wrong direction! It really doesn't matter at this stage; the object of the exercise just now is to get the wheel in continuous motion—to get the feel of it.

After a while you are almost bound to press (I call it 'pump', from the days when I had a foot pump for the tyres on my van)—you are almost bound to pump at the wrong moment, and the wheel will, after rocking from side to side as you attempt to get in phase again, stop. Now you can rotate the crank to 2 o'clock and start off again. You will soon find that in, say, 10 to 15 minutes, you can keep the wheel rotating and that out-of-phase pumps get rarer and rarer. But keep going; keep on treadling until your ankle aches, and then leave the wheel alone as you relax at some other job for an hour or so.

It may be that when you return you will be right back where you started, but that state of affairs will not last for very long, and you will soon be treadling away happily. When you first start you will probably find it easier to maintain a fairly fast rate of pumping, maybe in excess of 80 a minute, but it is desirable, indeed necessary, for us to be able to treadle as slowly as possible. So see how slowly you can pump and still keep the wheel rotating; see if you can get it down to one pump a second, and finally down to 40 pumps a minute.

We want a slow, soothing, gentle motion, as slow as we can manage, and we want to be able to keep this up for indefinite periods.

But stop a moment. There is another aspect I would like you to consider now. We have described our equipment as a twisting machine. Now we want to discover just how much twist it imparts for every pump of the treadle.

To do that, turn the crank until it is at BDC; apply a little tension to the drive band to ensure that there is no slippage and turn the flyer so that the arms are vertical. Tie a bow of wool or a piece of string around the top arm, just a loop so that it will not fall off. Now, slowly turning the wheel by hand, count the number of times the marked arm of the flyer comes up to the top during one complete revolution of the crank, from BDC to BDC. Make sure you have it right; do it again, to leave no doubt. You must be dead accurate, for on this figure will depend the quality and type of yarn your machine is best able to produce.

Ratios vary tremendously—that is, the ratio of spindle whorl to wheel diameter, which determines how many times the spindle will revolve for each revolution of the wheel. Satisfactory worsted yarn for weft or knitting can be produced by inserting 6 TPI, that is, if the wheel has a 6:1 ratio, allowing one inch of fibre to be twisted for each revolution of the wheel, equal, with one pump a second, to a production rate of 5 feet (1·5 m) of yarn a minute, or 100 yards (91 m) an hour. A ratio of 10:1 makes things a little more difficult, for it would, at 1 inch (2·5 cm) of fibre for each pump, produce a rather hard yarn, one best suited for warp. A softer yarn for weft or knitting could be made by twisting 2 inches of fibre at each pump of the treadle, equal to 5 TPI. That is quite manageable for the more experienced spinner. It may sound easy to present 2 inches (5 cm) of fibre to the wheel at each pump of the treadle, but remember it must be an accurate 2 inches, and the ability to draw out (draft) 2 inches of a stated quantity of fibre a second will demand considerable practice, and a quite high standard of roving.

At a 15:1 ratio, 1 inch of fibre a pump would result in a hard yarn, similar to that required in our example of a warp thread; 2 inches, equal to $7\frac{1}{2}$ TPI, would give us a fairly hard yarn, perhaps a little soft for warp and too hard for knitting, but ideal for the weft we discussed earlier; 3 inches (7.6 cm), equal to 5 TPI, gives a yarn soft enough for knitting, but 3 inches of fibre drafted every second is a job for an expert.

A ratio of 20:1 is not uncommon, especially on some of the older Scandinavian wheels. It is, I think, too high a twist ratio for use with comfort for worsted spinning and had better be reserved for short fibre spinning. Such a wheel would need a fresh spindle whorl to be made, to bring it down to an acceptable ratio before it could be used for the type of work we have in mind.

In passing, it is perhaps worth mentioning that no one wheel of fixed ratio can cope with an infinitely variable range of fibres and yarns, but that it is a relatively easy matter, once you know the twist requirements of your yarns, to have a new whorl made so that your wheel is able to produce those you require most of with the minimum of effort. The converse, too, is true, that knowing the ratio of a wheel will enable you to select yarns it is able to produce comfortably.

Let us assume that every time you pump the treadle, every time the wheel completes one revolution, the spindle rotates 6 times. That means that every time you pump the treadle you are inserting 6 twists into the yarn you are making.

If, for every pump of the treadle, you allow one inch of fibre to be fed to the machine, you will produce a yarn of 6 twists per inch (6 TPI). If, for every pump of the treadle, you allow $1\frac{1}{2}$ inches of fibre to be twisted, then that will give you the equivalent of 4 TPI; 2 inches of fibre = 3 TPI; $\frac{1}{2}$ inch = 12 TPI; $\frac{3}{4}$ inch = 8 TPI, and so on. To get 6 TPI from a wheel with an 18:1 ratio would require 3 inches of fibre fed to the spindle at each pump of the treadle.

So important is this aspect of spinning in relation to yarn quality that I want you to get it indelibly fixed in your brain that every time you pump the treadle you are inserting a set amount of twist in a given quantity of fibre.

So, after removing the mark from the flyer, start the treadle again, but this time, every time you pump the treadle say, mentally, '6 ... 6 ... 6 ... 6 ... 6 ... 6 ... 6 ... 6 ... 6' or whatever the number may be. Yes, I know it sounds a little silly, but do it nonetheless.

Treadling will be getting easier, more rhythmic, slower all the time, 6 .... 6 .... 6 .... 6, until in a couple of days of odd half-hours 6 ..... 6 ..... 6 ..... 6, you will have reached the stage where you can sit down, turn the wheel to 2 o'clock and start off treadling 6 ...... 6 ...... 6, without any bother at all.

It is particularly important that, if the wheel stops for any reason at all when under spinning conditions, the bobbin and flyer should not rotate backwards, even if the wheel accidentally does, for that will cause the yarn on the bobbin to unwind and probably snarl up on the hooks. So always rest your left hand on the bobbin and flyer unit if the wheel stops.

The next stage is to use our twisting machine for the purpose for which it was made. Let us start by attaching to the bobbin a 3-foot (1 m) length of fairly fine commercially made yarn. Tie it on the bobbin and pull the other end through the hollow spindle with a crooked piece of wire, pulling the whole 3 feet through. You will be well advised to tie a piece of crooked wire to your machine at some point, for it will be in constant use. We use plastic-coated garden wire; it is easy to bend into a crook, and since the crooks always seem to be getting lost, a reel from which to make new ones is a necessity.

Loop the yarn up over the arm of the flyer adjacent to the hole by which the yarn enters the spindle, from where it will be guided down on to the bobbin by the hooks. Rotate the bobbin in the same direction as the wheel a couple of times to ensure that the yarn is properly attached, and then, holding the yarn gently between finger and thumb of your left hand about

2 inches (5 cm) away from the spindle, turn the crank to 2 o'clock and start treadling slowly. It may be necessary here to adjust the tension slightly, so that as the spindle rotates, the yarn is drawn in through the hollow end and wound on to the bobbin. With the bobbin empty, a very slight tension will probably suffice.

You will see that as the yarn is drawn into the spindle, between your finger and thumb, it is rotating in the same direction as the spindle and as the wheel. Because, when the wheel turns in a clockwise direction, the twisted fibres in the yarn are inclined towards the right, it is called a 'Z' twist, the stroke of the 'Z' being in the same direction as the angle of the fibre. When the wheel turns in an anti-clockwise direction the fibres are inclined towards the left and produce an 'S' twist.

Stop the wheel before the yarn disappears into the spindle, or if you did not stop soon enough, pull the yarn out with your crooked wire, pull the yarn back, all 3 feet of it. The resistance to your pull must not be great—the belt over the bobbin should exert slight resistance but not make the pulling out a strain on the yarn. It must not, of course, unwind unchecked; if it will just unwind with a standard 200-g or 8 oz weight suspended from the yarn, it will be just about right (Fig. 93).

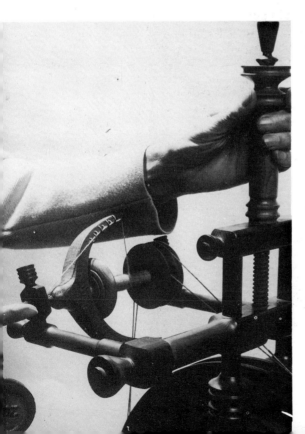

Fig. 93 Attach an 8-oz (226-g) weight to the end of the yarn, support it over one finger, close to the spindle so that the yarn runs freely, and adjust the tension so that the bobbin will just unwind of its own accord.

Before we again try the winding-on movement, tie a knot somewhere near the centre of the length of yarn and try the following experiments.

First lay the yarn over a ruler, with the knot against an inch mark, then, with the yarn transporting arm of the flyer vertical, rotate the wheel by hand so that the flyer revolves one complete revolution. Now check to see how much yarn has been wound on. If the length is around 3 inches, then that is very satisfactory, because it means that you can wind on 3 inches of yarn in which only one turn of twist has been inserted. It could mean that, if your bobbin core is of $\frac{1}{2}$-inch (1·3 cm) diameter (equivalent to about $1\frac{1}{2}$-inch (3·8 cm) circumference), then the bobbin rotates twice to the spindle's once (Figs 94 and 95).

If, however, the wind-on is only $\frac{1}{2}$ to 1 inch (or about 2 cm) for each

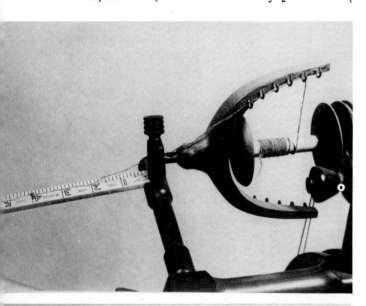

Fig. 94   Knot the yarn so that it is clearly seen, turn the flyer until one arm is vertical, place a ruler against the spindle and the knot against an inch mark . . . then rotate the wheel slowly so that the flyer makes one complete revolution.

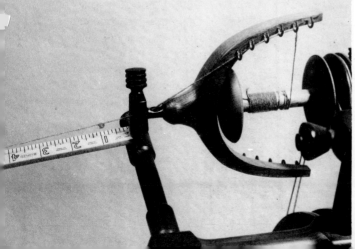

Fig. 95   The number of inches the knot moves along the ruler will indicate the amount of yarn that can be wound on for each revolution of the spindle— a piece of vital information.

revolution of the flyer, this can lead either to over-twisting, because the yarn gets additional twist inserted during the slow wind-on if a long draft is being used (woollen-spinning only); or it leads to under-twisting if a short draft, because part of the twisting cycle has to be used for winding on.

In woollen spinning the long draw method is often described where the spinner draws out 2 or 3 feet (0·6–1 m) of yarn over a given number of pumps of the treadle, producing a yarn of known and repeatable length and twist content. After twist insertion, the spinner winds the yarn on; ideally the whole length should wind on with very little extra twist added. But with a slow wind-on, many extra twists may be inserted. More importantly, the twist distribution is uneven down the length of yarn because that part which is past the spindle ceases to be twisted whilst that to be wound on is still receiving twists. The result is a harsh, over-spun yarn.

Moreover, these conditions change as the bobbin fills, because as the yarn is wound on so the diameter of the bobbin core increases—a bobbin core of $\frac{1}{2}$-inch (1·3 cm) diameter will wind on approximately $1\frac{1}{2}$ inches (4 cm) of yarn for each revolution, but when it is built up to 1-inch diameter it will wind on approximately 3 inches (7·6 cm); at $1\frac{1}{2}$-inch diameter it will wind on $4\frac{1}{2}$ inches (11·4 cm) every time it revolves. Because the increase in bobbin diameter increases the wind-on rate, the twist content of the yarn falls—less additional twist is being inserted in the now speeded-up wind-on. The yarn gets softer, and the spinner feels more confident, saying 'Ah, I've got the hang of this now!' and spins away merrily until the bobbin is filled and replaced by an empty one, whereupon the trouble reappears. This the spinner attempts to correct by a little twiddle here, a little twist there, and the odd blasphemous comment. Many, many times I have had spinners complain that 'I have a lovely wheel, but it is *so* temperamental', when really they are both at fault because not only is the wheel wrongly made, but if the spinner knew the job, the fault would be recognized for what it was.

In worsted spinning, the fault can produce a softer yarn than originally intended, because the roving is drawn out in controlled lengths and twisted and wound on in the space of one revolution of the wheel. If an inch (2·5 cm) of fibre is presented to the spindle, and if it takes two revolutions of the spindle to wind it on, the yarn will receive rather less twist than if the total number of spindle revolutions were used for twisting and the yarn wound on in a fraction of a revolution. In this case, the yarn would become slightly harder spun as the bobbin filled, because the increase in wind-on rate would enable all the spindle revolutions to be used for twisting.

117

It is a simple fault to correct. All that is necessary is to have the groove in the bobbin deepened to about half that of the spindle whorl, if that is at all possible. A poor alternative is to fill the bobbin with yarn until it achieves a reasonable wind-on rate, and then cover the yarn with gummed paper, using that as a new bobbin core. True, you will have lost some, perhaps considerable, bobbin capacity, but that left will at least be filled with yarn spun under more uniform conditions.

To get back to our experiment, if the yarn take-up on an empty bobbin is, say, 3 inches for one revolution of the flyer, this would mean that 1 inch of yarn would be wound on for every $\frac{1}{3}$ revolution of the spindle—a truly insignificant amount out of the 6 revolutions we get from each pump of the treadle, for it means that of the 6 revolutions no less than $5\frac{2}{3}$ are used for twisting, the other $\frac{1}{3}$ being taken up with winding on the one inch of yarn that has been made. This represents the maximum time that one inch of yarn will take to wind on, for, as the bobbin fills and the core diameter increases, so more yarn will be capable of being wound on at each revolution. But since we always start with an empty bobbin, it will be *that* wind-on rate which is important and must be maintained if our yarns are to be uniform.

If you grip the yarn by the knot, between thumb and finger of the left hand, and turn the crank to 2 o'clock and start treadling, you will feel your hand being drawn towards the spindle. It is easy to resist the pull; it is, after all, only 200 g (7 oz) or so. Do so, and keep treadling slowly. With no wind-on taking place, twist will accumulate between your hand and the spindle. Stop the wheel and you can see that the yarn is tightly twisted. When the hand is moved towards the spindle, that is, when the tension is taken off, the yarn snarls up and coils about itself. Compare it with the yarn on the other side of your finger and thumb, the part which no twist reached because of the barrier they formed. Here, the yarn is soft and relaxed (Fig. 96).

Fig. 96   Yarn twisted between the spindle and thumb, but the twist prevented from passing between the finger and thumb into the relaxed yarn by the slight pressure they exert.

That part of the yarn occupies the position that will presently be occupied by the roving, an area in which twist, apart from that previously inserted when the roving was made, is prohibited.

Twist is inserted in the fibre, turning it into a yarn, by the spindle; the quantity of fibre allowed to be twisted is controlled by the hands, and I think that, for once in their lives, left-handed people are at a slight advantage over their much more plentiful relations, for the left-handed spinner holds the roving in the left hand and pulls out the fibre (drafts) with the right, the fibre feed taking place in line with the spindle orifice. A right-handed person holds the roving in the right hand and drafts with the left, the fibre entering the orifice at a considerable angle from the right. None of which matters in the slightest if that is the comfortable way for you to sit and work! (Fig 97).

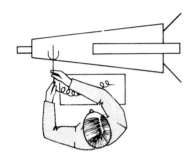

Fig. 97(a) Feeding the spindle with fibre from the right hand, roving held in left hand.

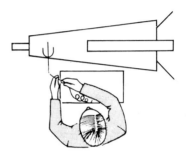

Fig. 97 (b) Feeding the spindle with fibre from the left hand, roving held in right hand.

If you are ambidextrous try both methods and see which you prefer. If you are totally right-handed you may only be comfortable working system B. If you are not too badly right-handed and can comfortably work system A, then I would advise you to do so. It seems tidier and more practical.

In one hand, then, is held the roving; between the thumb and finger of the other hand is the meeting point where the untwisted fibre of the roving becomes twisted into a yarn by the twist travelling down the yarn between the spindle eye and the finger and thumb.

That area between the two hands where the fibre is still untwisted is used to regulate the amount of fibre that will form the yarn. In an automatic spinning machine it would be called the 'drafting zone'—which is more convenient than saying 'that area where the roving is attenuated to the density required for the count being spun'.

On the spinning machine the roving is guided to, and passes between, a series of pairs of horizontal rollers, the bottom roller usually being driven, the top roller acting as a weight (Fig 98). The front pair of rollers—those nearest the spindle—are arranged to rotate faster than the rear pair, so that the fibres caught up between them are drawn out and separated from the mass behind, thus producing the required thinning (drafting) of the roving to spinning proportions.

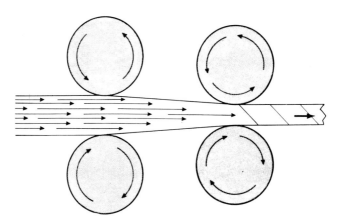

Fig. 98   The front rollers (right) *rotate faster than the rear rollers, drawing out and attenuating the fibre so that a constant amount is presented for spinning.*

The finger and thumb of the hand nearest the spindle can be likened to the front rollers, and the hand holding the roving to the rear pair.

Since by inserting twist into the fibre mass we force the fibres together, so uniting their individual strength and producing a yarn in which inter-fibre slippage is minimal, it follows that if the thinning down of the roving is to take place, no twist must be allowed to enter the drafting zone. So here is a major requirement of the drafting finger and thumb. They must not allow any twist from their spinning side to enter the drafting side. The rollers do it by constantly rotating and drawing in new fibre, the weight or pressure of the top roller preventing any twist passing beneath it into the drafting zone.

120

Your finger and thumb will use pressure in the same way—just go back to your wheel again; pull out a length of yarn and let it dangle so that all the twist can run out. Now hold the end in the roving hand and pinch the yarn with the drafting hand, say some 6 inches (15 cm) from the spindle (first having turned the crank to 2 o'clock). Now pump the treadle a few times. Twist will build up at A, but area B, the drafting zone, will be relaxed. Now relax pressure on the drafting finger and thumb, but not so much that twist can pass between them, and gently slide that hand towards the roving fingers. You will observe the twist following the drafting fingers along the yarn, increasing area A and reducing area B, but—and here is the important thing—not allowing any twist to precede the drafting fingers into area B (Fig. 99).

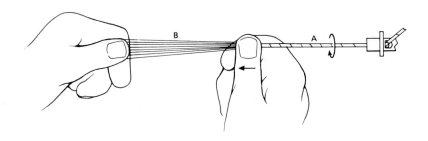

Fig. 99   As the spindle rotates, twist is inserted in the yarn, area A, but must not be allowed to pass between the finger and thumb into area B.

As we have seen, in roller drafting the roving is drawn in between rollers and, because the front pair rotate faster than the rear pair, is attenuated by them.

This attenuation is achieved by our hands in a very similar manner—in fact, of course, you and I are now reversing history, for the drafting rollers were developed to copy the action of the spinner's hands, and we are now seeking to re-learn the spinner's hand action by using the rollers as an example!

The action of the roving hand will be to keep a constant supply of roving to be drafted, at the same time guiding stray fibre and applying such pressure (tension) as may be necessary.

Since our fingers are unable to revolve, we achieve similar results by a rolling action with the ball of the thumb, coupled with a reciprocal motion of the drafting hand, between the spindle and the roving hand.

Diagrams 1 and 2 in Fig. 100 show the drafting hand sliding up the drafting zone followed by the twist.

Diagram 3—drafting hand reaches roving hand, drafting fingers roll open and on closing pinch fresh quantity of fibres, but never relaxing pressure sufficiently to allow twist to pass between finger and thumb and to enter the drafting zone.

In Diagram 4, drafting hand moves towards spindle, allowing yarn previously twisted to be wound on and drawing out fresh fibres to be twisted.

Diagram 5 shows drafting hand almost at limit of drafting stroke, when it will re-commence the sequence as at Diagram 1.

Fig. 100   Drafting action.

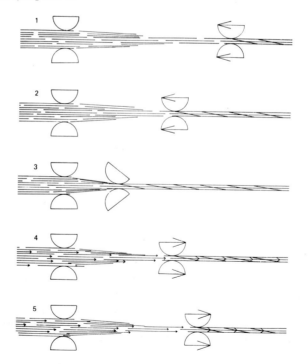

In practice, the roving extends some distance in front of the roving hand, presenting a tuft or cone of fibres to the drafting fingers. The small amount of twist present in the roving tends to spiral the fibres it contains into a cone shape, especially under the slight additional pressure or pull of the drafting action, so that a reasonably constant fibre mass is presented to the drafting fingers.

The action of the drafting fingers is rather delicate, but an easy one to acquire. Pressure control is vitally important and varies considerably over the sequence of operations. It is greatest after nipping a fresh supply of fibres and drawing them away from the roving hand; it eases as the drafting fingers slide down the untwisted attenuated fibre in the drafting zone, but never to the extent that twist can slip between the drafting fingers and precede them into the drafting zone.

As experience is gained, the point of twist can be made to take place right between the ball of the finger and thumb. This is ideal because it tends to fold in any fibre ends that are able to escape the contour of the yarn and so improves the thready, lustrous appearance which is one of the main characteristics of the true worsted yarn.

Under ideal conditions, the distance between the roving hand and the spindle is a constant. So, too, is the distance from the roving hand that the drafting hand moves (Fig. 101).

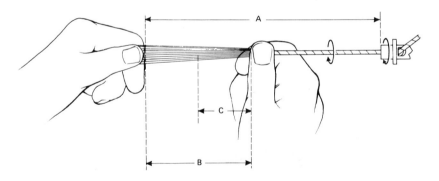

Fig. 101   The constants. Ideally, distance A between the roving hand and the spindle should be a constant. Distance B represents the maximum movement away from the roving hand, C the nearest. BC will then represent the drafting stroke which, for a given yarn, should never vary.

Now, if the draft is a constant and the amount of fibre drafted is a constant, and one complete drafting cycle takes place with every pump of the treadle, the result must be a yarn of uniform fibre content and distribution, uniform diameter and uniform twist content. *These are the major requirements for the components of any high quality fabric.*

Of course, you will not achieve such perfection in five minutes, but with constant practice you will in as many days. *Of course* your ankle will ache, *of course* your drafting fingers will ache, and your brain will reel as you attempt to synchronize fingers and foot. The world is full of people who drop out when the going gets tough, but not you, please. The awkward phase only lasts a few days and we should be silly to deny its existence—but think of the feeling of satisfaction when you are over the hump and coasting confidently down the other side.

Having discussed the basic principles, let us see how well we can apply them in practice. First of all, if we are going to control accurately the fibre in the drafting zone, it is essential that you can see the fibre clearly—try spinning an undyed wool roving in a room with a white tiled floor and you will see what I mean. Similarly, spinning a dark brown fibre on a brown rug can cause unnecessary eye strain. So always arrange things so that the background against which you view the fibre you are spinning is of a contrasting colour.

The roving hand can form a very efficient delivery shute to the drafting zone by curving the fingers towards the palm and laying the thumb over the middle joint of the index finger on that hand, the roving passing between the two (Fig. 102).

You will probably modify the action of the drafting fingers as you progress. Initially, you may pinch between the tip of the index finger and the ball of the thumb, the pinching being made by a sort of rolling action of both thumb and finger. Later you may find your drafting hand altering position slightly, with the thumb and forefinger now resting about half-way down the second finger, with the palm about 45 degrees to the vertical and the remaining fingers straight to form a platform.

This platform provides a convenient background against which you can more clearly see the fibre. The fingers can also be called into play when odd bits of roving seem disinclined to join the drafted fibres to be twisted. Sometimes I find my thumb is resting across the middle joint of the index finger; the nipping or pinching of the fresh fibres is then accomplished by a rocking motion of the thumb. It works very well, providing an even larger platform of fingers against which the fibres can rest or be seen. It is not a

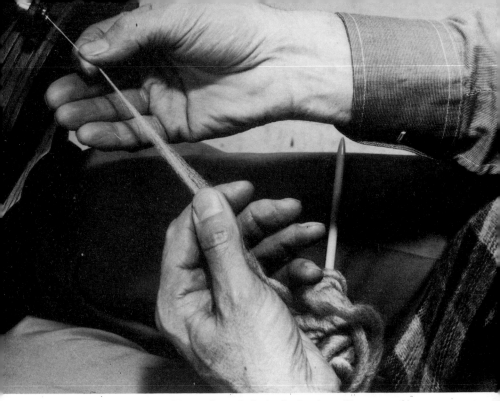

Fig. 102   A 'spinner's eye view'. The roving spindle in the lap (unrolling upwards), the roving passing up over the palm of the left hand, the index finger and thumb providing a tensioning device and quantity control. Then the fibre passes into the drafting zone, is attenuated and passes between the drafting fingers to be twisted into a yarn. Note how the fingers of the drafting hand form a convenient platform against which the drafted fibre is clearly seen.

position in which I consciously start, but it seems to develop after pro-longed spinning, perhaps as the ball of the index finger tires.

I must emphasize what you will already have realized—that it is difficult to say that this procedure is correct and that one is wrong. The right one for you is the one that is the most comfortable—the one that enables you to produce the highest quality yarns. Having found it, stick to it, do not be influenced by people who say 'but the correct way is like *this*'. It may well be, for them; but you are *you* and so always use *your* method, provided it enables you to produce a true worsted yarn of consistent quality. What does it matter then if you are left-handed or whether you pinch with your index finger or your second finger?

Before we start talking of possible snags, let us briefly go over the important points again.

1   If your yarn is going to be uniform in twist content you *must* know how much twist your wheel produces, *and* how much twist you require in your yarn. (See Chapter 8.)

2   The easiest method of ensuring that the twist insertion is accurate is to arrange for your wheel to revolve the spindle the required number of revolutions at each pump of the treadle, even if that means that a new spindle whorl has to be made.

3   Make sure that you are capable of delivering the required amount of fibre to the spindle for each pump of the treadle. For example, 6 TPI is easy if the spindle revolves 6 times at each pump of the treadle and you feed the spindle with one inch of fibre, but very difficult if it revolves 18 times to each pump, requiring 3 inches (7·6 cm) of fibre, a near-impossible amount to supply with the accuracy required, except for the very experienced, and heartbreakingly difficult for the beginner—a task which should not be attempted.

4   Ensure that your bobbin can wind on extremely rapidly *when empty* the total amount of yarn twisted at each pump of the treadle.

5   Allow the twist to enter the drafted fibres between the ball of the thumb and drafting finger, so that the fibre ends are all, or mostly, tucked in the strand, giving the smooth, thready, lustrous appearance for which worsted yarns are famed.

6   Never allow the twist to pass into the drafting zone.

7   Use your hands like the drafting rollers, one to feed fibre into the drafting zone, one to extend or separate the amount of fibre to be spun to give a yarn of the required diameter.

So, let us now make a start on some practical tests, aiming for a yarn of about $\frac{1}{30}$ inch (0·8 mm) diameter.

Our first requirement is to join or attach the roving to the spinning-wheel. The purist may spin a length of yarn from the roving in exactly the same way as the roving was made, by using a knitting needle and, after first twisting a few fibres between finger and thumb to give a start, winding the thread on to the needle and spinning a couple of feet of yarn off the point. The only thing to watch is that the direction of twist is the same as that of the spindle on the wheel.

Having produced a couple of feet of thread, you take the end off the needle and, holding it to ensure that the twist does not run out, thread one end through the hollow point of the spindle, over the arm of the flyer and secure it to the bobbin; turn the bobbin a few revolutions in its normal direction of rotation to make sure that the yarn is gripping.

A much simpler method is to cut off a 2-foot (0·6 m) length of machine-spun thread, attach it to the bobbin, pass it up over the flyer and out through the spindle eye, and attach the roving to that. In any case, most of you will already have a length of yarn attached to the bobbin from the experiments we conducted earlier, so we might as well make use of that.

The only remaining problem is to attach the end of the roving to the yarn. My method is to open out the end of the yarn into an untwisted mass if at all possible—if the yarn is two-ply it is sometimes easier to do, and then to divide the mass into two, so that the yarn end looks like a hairy 'Y'. Make each arm of the 'Y' about 1½ inches (4 cm) long.

The end of the roving is pulled out until a web of fibre, roughly equal to the quantity estimated for the required yarn, extends in front of the roving hand by about three inches—you can easily determine how much fibre is needed by twisting it between finger and thumb. If you have pulled out too much you can pull out fibre from the front of that, but if too little, giving a thin, weak strand, pull them right out and start again.

The thinned-out end of the roving is placed between the arms of the 'Y', the arms are smoothed down and the joint held between finger and thumb of the roving hand (Fig. 103).

Fig. 103   End of yarn opened out for joining. Note the manner in which the two ends are held.

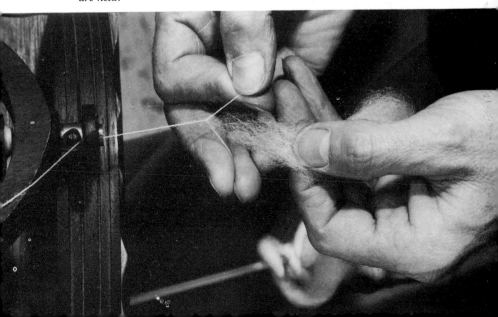

The free hand starts the wheel and is then immediately transferred to a point about halfway down the joint.

The roving hand slips back along the roving to take up control at the point where the roving is drafted.

Very quickly the influence of the twist will be felt; the yarn will be seen to be revolving between spindle and drafting hand. Watch closely, and you will see the arms of the 'Y' close down and pinch the end of the roving in the twisting action.

It is now, when the roving is firmly attached to the thread, that the thumb and forefinger of the drafting hand (hereinafter called the DH) is slid down the drafting zone. The twist will follow them down and the joint will be twisted into an integral part of the thread.

The DH slides up to the RH (roving hand), nips a fresh supply of fibre, draws it out 1 inch (2·5 cm) (pump), then slides down the fibre just drawn out, followed by the twist, nips more fibre, draws it out an inch (pump), slides down the fibre (followed by the twist), nips fresh, draws it out an inch (pump) and so on, and on. A steady, synchronized movement of hand and foot—one complete sequence for every revolution of the wheel, 1 inch of fibre for every six revolutions of the spindle (Figs 104 and 105), or whatever the ratio is on your wheel.

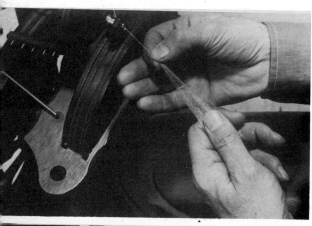

Fig. 104 The D.H. has made the drafting stroke (corresponding to 4, Fig. 100); the yarn has been wound on and the D.H. is about to slide down the drafted fibre towards the R.H.

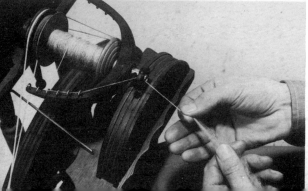

Fig. 105 The drafted fibre has been twisted into a yarn, and the D.H. is about to pinch fresh fibre to draw it out of the R.H. (No. 3, Fig. 100), and then return to the position in Fig. 104.

If you can master that, you are on the way, but you will never produce a uniform thread if you do not. It is only a knack and will come in time; as we have said before, think of all those spinners of two centuries ago who did it as a matter of course—and then settle down to some solid practice.

One of the main causes of failure is that instead of *sliding* the DH down the yarn, the spinner releases the yarn and moves the hand down towards the RH to re-pinch the roving, only to find that the fibres will no longer draw out and that the roving has become locked (Fig. 106).

What has happened is that the moment the spinner lets go of the yarn the twist leaps ahead of the DH fingers, twists the fibres in the drafting zone and, entering the roving, twists the fibres there as well. In no time at all sufficient fibres are influenced for inter-fibre slippage, i.e. drafting, to become impossible.

Fig. 106   Instead of sliding *down the drafted fibre, the D.H. fingers have let go of the yarn, whereupon the twist was able to pass ahead of them and lock the drafting zone fibres. Compare with the drafting zone of Fig. 104.*

If that happens, the solution is to stop the wheel, grip the yarn firmly at the point where it enters the roving, and rotate the roving in the opposite direction, so that the fibres can unwind. That will probably entail lifting the roving needle from your lap and rotating the whole unit, roving, needle and all, until the fibres adjacent to the drafting zone can again be pulled apart. If that is not possible, then instead of releasing the roving, try to rotate its end in the same direction to that of the spindle, at the same time rotating the end of the yarn in the opposite direction to the spindle rotation. This will untwist the fibres in the end of the roving sufficiently for slippage to occur and allow drafting to recommence.

Before starting the wheel again, slide the DH down towards the RH, allowing the twist which has accumulated in the yarn to run out into the drafted fibre as it follows the DH. Nip some fresh fibres, draw them out, release your hold on the roving and start the wheel with that hand. It must be admitted that right-handed spinners are at a slight advantage here, for it is marginally easier to start the wheel if the RH is the right hand than if it is the left. The left-hander very quickly gets into the way of doing the same thing rather differently; for instance, I release the roving and rotate the wheel with my left hand. Others, I have noticed, transfer the RH to pinch the yarn immediately in front of the DH, and use the DH to start the wheel, then replace the DH to the drafting position and the RH back on the roving.

It sounds more complicated to read than to do. Again, the answer is practice. Practise stopping and starting the wheel with the roving attached until your procedure is an unthought-about, effortless routine.

Twist running into the roving can only occur if you allow twist to pass between the DH fingers into the drafting zone. The answer is obvious— *never* relax completely the pressure on the drafting fingers. You will quickly discover the pressure to apply—too much is unnecessary and will only make the fingers ache and the process an unpleasant chore. You can see when the twist starts to involve the fibres in the drafting zone—you require just sufficient pressure to prevent that happening.

Another problem which often arises is associated with the drafting zone itself. Ideally, the hands should always work a set distance apart and, with a roving of absolute uniformity, it might be possible to state a distance, but in practice the rovings vary somewhat in fibre distribution—there are thick and thin places. There shouldn't be, but there are! Of course, as you gain more experience, the quality of your rovings will improve, but it is unlikely that you will ever completely eradicate these variations.

The effect of a thin place in a roving is to cause these fibres to become more twisted than those in a thicker place—twist will pile up or accumulate there when the sliver is made into a roving, rather than be evenly distributed over the whole area of the roving, although this can, to some extent, be controlled by winding on the thin patch if you see it coming in time, before much twist has entered it.

The effect that the excess of twist has on the thin area of the roving is not wholly bad, for it tends to make it draw out (draft) rather more evenly than the fibres in the thicker areas. This happens because, as you apply tension to draw out the fibres, it has the effect of compacting the fibres in the roving, pushing them more closely together. The drafted fibres more easily pull others along with them, and you find that the web of fibre in the drafting zone can be maintained to the desired density with ease, but that the physical effort involved in drafting is considerably greater.

For some reason which is difficult to explain, when that situation arises I have noticed that, like many of the students I have taught, I tend to draw out more fibre than I am feeding to the spindle, say $1\frac{1}{2}$ inches (4 cm) per treadle pump. But I still only feed the required amount to the spindle, which means that the drafting zone steadily extends—the hands getting further and further apart (Fig. 107).

Fig. 107   If the fibres in the drafting zone thin drastically, there may no be solution but to pull the zone apart, form a Y in the end of the yarn, and start again.

When the thin place is almost worked out, the fibre in the following thicker part of the roving does not pull out to anything like the same extent because the twist concentration is less, which means that the fibres are not so closely bunched together and the moving fibres will not so readily drag others along with them. Unless something is done, a thin patch will occur in the yarn where the number of fibres drafted fell off.

But, if your DH is now, say, 4 inches (10 cm) away from the coned tip of the roving, what do you do? Well, without drafting any more fibre, you slide your DH down the drafted fibres one inch to the pump, at the same time moving *both* hands one inch towards the spindle so that the yarn twisted can be wound on. Repeat the movement until the excess of drafted fibre has been twisted, whereupon the normal pinching-drafting motion can be resumed. If the fibres had thinned drastically at the point where they leave the roving a thin, weak place in the yarn is inevitable, and the only solution then is to break the yarn on the spindle side of the weak point, make a 'Y' in the end of the yarn and rejoin with the correctly drafted quantity of fibre.

The solution of the problem is in two parts: (a) produce as uniform a roving as you can, and (b) be careful not to draft more fibre than is required for each pump of the treadle.

Although I have stressed the importance of not allowing twist to precede the DH into the drafting zone, some twist will inevitably be present, because the sliver was twisted to turn it into a roving, and we have just seen how this twist in the roving holds the fibres together and aids drafting.

So perhaps that statement should be modified to 'some small amount of twist is permissible in the drafting zone, but it *must come from the roving, NOT THE YARN*'.

If the twist content of the roving is low, the manner in which the fibres spiral as they are drafted will not be so pronounced. This can lead to a gradual fall-off in the amount of fibre extracted at each drafting action, with a consequent thinning of the yarn. Matters can be improved if the end of the roving is turned or rotated gently to insert some additional twist.

It sounds difficult to describe, but is, in fact, very easy to do. You simply turn the end of the roving that is passing out between the finger and thumb of the RH in the opposite direction from that of the spindle rotation; you do this by rolling it down the index finger with the thumb. In all probability, a turn or two will be sufficient to close the fibres into the desired cone-shaped point with the fibres spiralling slightly towards the RH. You can also put additional twist into the roving by rotating the roving spindle, of course.

132

This will compact the fibres and uniform drafting should again become possible.

There are, however, some occasions when a little twist has to be inserted in the drafted fibre from the DH. For it sometimes happens, especially when the twist content of the roving is very low, that the end of the roving will not form a cone but is a tuft of separate fibres, the outer ones of which are very difficult to catch with the DH.

What usually happens then is that the DH nips the centre fibres and pulls them out. Adjacent fibres move with them but, their ends being free, they tend to ruck up on the next drafting stroke and, unless the stray ends can be caught up in the twist, a hairy, whiskery slub may result, because the orderliness of the roving has been disturbed.

The root cause, of course, is the lack of twist in the roving, probably because the roving was uneven in density—a thing you will try to avoid in the future, but the knowledge of which does not help you much now. Our problem is how to capture the static outer fibres of the roving tip, to get them involved in the twist, and get them moving once more.

The first step is to compress the end to a point, by moving the RH up to the end of the roving. The next stage is to capture the outer fibres—difficult to do by pinching alone, much easier if some twist is present—not so much that we jam up the works, just sufficient to involve the fibres and start them on a drafting course.

To allow twist to pass under the thumb from the spindle is easy; you simply relax the pressure of the thumb, but it is difficult to control, for twist can run into the roving like wildfire.

It is far more controllable to insert twist by twisting the drafted fibres under the DH fingers—simply by rolling them between finger and thumb, inserting the twist in the same direction as that in the yarn. At the same time, some attempt must be made to compress the outer fibres of the roving by gently guiding them towards the twisted fibres in the drafting zone with the little finger or other fingers of the platform of the DH (Fig. 108).

Fig. 108   The drafting platform fingers about to be used to guide or compress the stray fibres in towards the finger and thumb of the D.H.

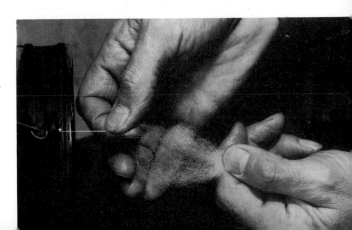

The inserted twist will involve some of the static fibres, which on the drafting stroke will move some adjacent to them, but the whole sequence may have to be repeated for two or three drafting strokes before the roving fibres are moving correctly again.

These distractions may cause your drafting and pumping to go awry, but try not to let it. They are extra jobs which have to be performed, when necessary, within the space of one pump, one drafting stroke.

If, in trying to sort out the problem, you carry on pumping without the drafting action, you will be adding extra twist to that length of yarn between the spindle and the DH. It would be better to stop the wheel altogether and sort out the trouble unhurriedly—when you can rotate the end of the roving or the drafted fibre as the case may be—and assess the results before starting the wheel again.

As we said, it may well take two or three pumps and drafting strokes to get it all sorted out, but you can do them in slow motion—rotating the wheel once by hand and making the necessary adjustments to the roving or to the drafting zone before rotating the wheel by hand again.

In extreme cases, when no amount of cajoling will sort out the situation, it may be best to break the thread, pull it out of the spindle until a piece of good quality yarn appears, insert more twist in the roving if necessary to get it right for drafting, then join the two and start spinning again (Fig. 109).

Fig. 109 Stop the wheel, pinch the yarn end of the drafting zone, and rotate the roving spindle to insert twist into the end of the roving.

These mistakes, snags and difficulties are all symptomatic of inexperience. It is because they exist and can be overcome that apprenticeships were necessary. You are not going to produce a perfect yarn the first day you sit at your wheel, but by understanding the process and its requirements you will be able to reason out the snags as they occur.

There are no short cuts. The only way to succeed is to practise, practise and practise—and bear in mind that you are doing what they rarely did in the days of the hand textile industry; you are attempting to be a 'one-man band', a wool-sorter, a dyer, a comber, a roving maker, a spinner. And added to that you already have those other skills by which you earn your daily bread.

It would, of course, be easier if one did, say, a solid month of combing followed by a similar period of roving making, etc. but that is impossible for most of us. We have to use the wool as we prepare it, or we would soon be unable to move for the stuff.

In a way, even that has its advantages, for having once used under-twisted roving you make very sure you do not repeat *that* mistake! And in varying the task from combing to spinning, the aches occasioned by one are dulled by those acquired by the other!

I find that acquiring a new skill usually has three distinct phases. At first one is very careful, each movement is controlled as it should be, concentration is a hundred per cent, and after a few initial snags the job goes well . . . dead easy . . . there's nothing in it . . . don't know what they make so much fuss about!

At this point we slide into phase two where, slightly over-confident, we allow our concentration to drop, our attention to wander. Snags occur which, with limited experience, take some sorting out, only to be followed by others, until we are so overwhelmed with correcting them that the basic requirements of the process are forgotten. But we won't be beaten, so we press on, get over-tired, nothing goes right, and we feel so humiliated that we are cross with ourselves and everyone about us.

The third phase comes after a rest from the task; we come back refreshed, relaxed, able to give the concentration any new skill requires, and things start to work properly again.

Phase two will probably return, but for ever-decreasing periods until, as you gain experience, it will disappear for ever. Once you realize that there is no short cut to experience, that it can only be gained by actually doing the job, and that the more you practise the sooner the aches, the snags, the frustrations will be over, then there remains only your determination that stands between you and a perfect length of worsted yarn.

Never lose sight of the fact that the whole purpose of the various processes we have been discussing is the production of a continuous length of yarn, as similar in its perfection as we can get it to those yarns produced in industry. In discussing the various ways to achieve this end, I have described methods which have proved workable and satisfactory to me, and to many people I have taught, but there is nothing hard or fast about it. If you can evolve a method which is more comfortable, less tiring for you, then that is the method you should adopt.

I cannot over-stress the fundamental importance of uniformity of twist and fibre content. Provided that you can ensure that your yarns are constant in these two vital factors, and provided that you can operate your machine with peace of mind and ease of body, the posture you adopt to do it is unimportant; it only becomes important if someone else attempts to copy you and finds it uncomfortable for them—but that is their problem, not yours. The temptation I feel we must resist at all costs is to imagine that what is right and comfortable for us must be equally comfortable for someone else.

Fig. 110   At rest. The roving spindle lodges neatly in the distaff socket.

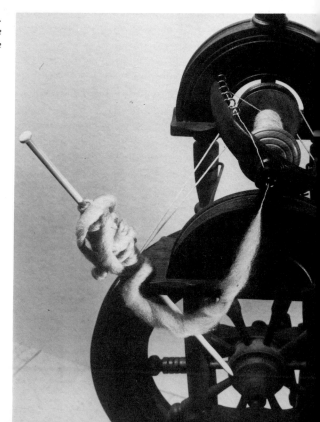

What is correct for you is probably determined by your body size, your muscle development—which is in turn governed by the type of work you do—the flexibility of your mind and fingers. But it is far too personal to you for you to say that your method—however successful you may be—is *the* correct method.

What I have attempted here is to show you the requirements of a yarn and my method of achieving the necessary standard. It is now for you to produce yarns with the qualities that are required for the specific end use you have in mind.

If you find that you can be comfortable using the methods and movement I have described, I shall be delighted, but I expect most of you will modify them in some way—because you are you, not me.

Do not become discouraged if things will not go right. Remember the first time you attempted to drive a car or ride a bicycle! If you get to the stage where things simply will not go right, leave it, abandon it, go for a walk or have a sleep—anything but carry on getting more and more tired and exasperated.

You will come back to it refreshed in mind and body. Your problems may still be there, but you will be in a better frame of mind to reason them out.

If you so understand the basic principles of the job that you can overcome the problems which arise by a process of reason, I shall feel that I have succeeded in my task.

The quality of your yarn will depend on the accurate control of the fibre being twisted and the accuracy of the twist insertion. The control of fibre being twisted will depend on the quality of your roving, its density, its twist content.

The quality of your roving will be governed by the standard of your sliver, which in turn will depend on the quality of your fleece, and how well you sorted it and prepared the fibres for combing.

The combing will be a pleasure if you made all your tools so well that they are a joy to handle.

Work, then, becomes something to which you look forward—and you never 'work' again!

Chapter 8
How Much Twist?

We have spent the previous chapters learning how to prepare the fibre for twisting, and then in how to control the twisting machine so that a definite and predictable amount of twist can be inserted in a given length of yarn. But how much twist is needed, and why should it vary?

As we have seen, it is easy to separate a bundle of loose fibres because the individual strands can slip past each other, but that quite a small amount of twist inserted into the fibre mass will force them together, when, because they are coiled about each other and their surface irregularities tend to interlock, it becomes more difficult for the fibres to separate. More twist may force the fibres so tightly together that no slippage at all is possible between them, and the individual strength of the separate fibres is united to form a twine the strength of which is roughly proportional to its fibre content.

There is no sudden change from easy separation of the fibres at low twist to complete lockage at high twist; it is a gradual process, the tendency of the fibres to slip past each other as the twist increases becoming less and less, until eventually it ceases altogether. That is the point of maximum strength. No amount of additional twist will increase it; in fact the reverse is more likely to be true, for still more twist may eventually weaken the yarn by causing individual fibres to break.

The twist insertion has also had an effect on the appearance of the fibre mass. Before twisting it was soft and fluffy but, as the twist was applied, it became more compact but still quite soft. More twist gave the mass a thread-like appearance, while still more emphasized the threadiness but made the twine harsh and unattractive to handle.

The amount of twist required to force a bundle of wool fibres together, so that they unite into a yarn, will depend on a number of factors—their length, quantity and individual diameter. A large bundle of fibre of given length and diameter would reach a stage of maximum strength with less twist in it than would be required in a small bundle of similar fibre, because there would be many more individual fibres in contact with each other— many more surfaces to grip.

The smaller bundle, having fewer fibres, would require more twist to force them together and hold them in contact. So the amount of twist required to give untwisted fibres the contour and character of a thread will depend upon the number of fibres involved, and the number of fibres involved will in turn govern the diameter of the yarn.

We have established, then, that the amount of twist inserted governs both the appearance and strength of the yarn. We shall now see that the amount of twist a yarn of given diameter receives above that which is necessary to force the fibres to unite into a thread is determined by its proposed end use. A warp thread, which has to withstand the abrasion caused by the heddles and the alternating tension as they are raised and lowered, will require considerable strength. The weft, on the other hand, needs to be soft so that it will flatten and give good cover, so will probably only need to be strong enough to withstand the drag of the shuttle. Since these two factors vary from loom to loom, weaver to weaver, cloth to cloth, it is impossible to say that all warp threads should have x amount of twist and all weft threads y. Hand-spinners tend to err on the safe side, giving plenty of twist = plenty of strength, judging the yarn by its feel and appearance.

The amount of twist required will depend on the type of fibre used, the yarn diameter and the type of fabric envisaged, but it should be possible for some guide to be given which would serve as a basis for experimental warps and weft containing enough twist for the proposed end use and no more.

This, in turn, should produce a more lively fabric and, equally important, *effectively increase the spinner's production since the twist that was previously wasted through over-twisting can now be used over a greater length of yarn.*

An experiment would not be completed until the fabric had been taken from the loom and finished, for low twist yarn has greater opportunity to shrink than yarns where the fibre has been tightly twisted.

The twist must be evenly distributed throughout the yarn. Uneven twist can cause many defects, thread breakage through weak places (low twist) or unmanageable yarns which snarl up, caused by high twist, uneven shrinkage, giving rise to an uneven or rucked fabric being amongst the most common.

There are two ways of visualizing twist. One is the way we have been discussing it, as a product of physically twisting the fibres to form a yarn. Another way would be to judge the twist by assessing the angle at which the fibres lie to the yarn axis. In a low twist yarn the fibres will spiral gradually up the length (Fig. 111), having perhaps an angle of 5 degrees to the axis. More twist would cause a tighter spiral (Fig. 112) and a greater twist angle.

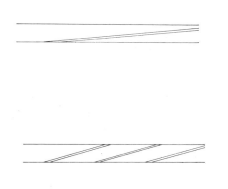

Fig. 111 A 5° twist angle—a soft yarn having perhaps only 2 TPI.

Fig. 112 A 15° twist angle, equal on the same scale to 5.9 TPI.

We have also seen that it will tend to discourage inter-fibre slippage, giving more strength but a harder feel. Still more twist produces an even tighter spiral (Fig. 113), a greater twist angle, considerably greater strength and a much harder yarn.

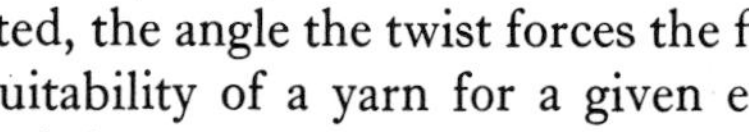

Fig. 113 A 25° twist angle equal to 10.5 TPI on the same scale.

We have, then, established a relationship between the amount of twist inserted, the angle the twist forces the fibres to assume to the yarn axis and the suitability of a yarn for a given end use—a high twist yarn to give strength in a warp would have a greater twist angle than a low twist yarn for soft weft filling, but both yarns could have the same diameter.

If now we had some ready means of relating twist angle to yarn diameter, and if some information relating yarn properties to twist angle were available, a useful guide to the amount of twist needed might emerge.

Fig. 114   Cross-section of a fabric woven on the square, where the
spaces between the warp threads are occupied by a
weft thread of equal diameter.

We know, or can easily obtain, the diameter of a yarn from those of
commerce. Most manufacturers give the loom settings required for their
yarns, how many threads per inch. But remember that to obtain the yarn
diameter the loom setting figure should be doubled because, in a square
fabric (one having as many picks to the inch as warp threads) a cross-
section would look something like Fig. 114, with the spaces between the
warp threads being occupied by a weft thread of equal diameter. A setting
of 20 threads to the inch will therefore indicate a yarn of $\frac{1}{40}$-inch (0·63 mm)
diameter. Another method of finding the yarn diameter is to cut a piece of
card (Fig. 115) measuring exactly 1 inch (2·5 cm) between the shoulders.
The yarn to be copied is wound on, setting each turn close to the previous
one, but not jammed up tight enough to reduce the cross-section by
flattening. When the space is filled, count the number of threads across the
card. The total number will give the fraction of an inch that each thread
occupies—40 threads (turns) will indicate a yarn of $\frac{1}{40}$-inch diameter.
You can also design your fabric to have the number of threads per inch
you personally prefer, of course (Appendix III).

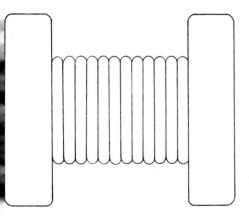

Fig. 115 Twelve turns of
thread have been wound
between the flanges of the
yarn gauge, a distance of ex-
actly 1 in (2.54 cm). There-
fore the yarn equals $\frac{1}{12}$-in
(2 mm) diameter.

Tables found in some old books on yarn properties give values related to twist angle. One such states that:

5° angle = a very soft twist
10° angle = a soft twist
15° angle = a soft medium twist
20° angle = a medium twist
25° angle = a hard medium twist
30° angle = a hard twist
45° angle = a very hard twist.
(See also Fig. 116.)

There are also formulae which enable you to relate the twist angle to the yarn diameter, giving as a quotient the twists per inch which the yarn might be expected to require. One such states:

$$\frac{\text{Diameter of yarn as a whole number}}{\pi \times \text{cotangent of longitudinal angle}} = \text{Twists per inch}$$

Fortunately we shall not be concerned with twist angles below 5 degrees or greater than 45 degrees, so to save a lot of unnecessary brain work I have worked out the $\pi \times$ cotangent of longitudinal angle for the most significant of the intermediate degrees and given them in a table at the end of the book (Appendix II).

We are now in a position to determine the amount of twist required for both the warp and weft threads as the basis of an experimental length of fabric. A 40 threads per inch setting indicates a yarn of $\frac{1}{80}$-inch diameter. For the warp, requiring strength and therefore a hard twist, we might select an angle of 30 degrees. Our table gives the product of π and the cotangent of 30 degrees as 5·44 which divided into 80 = 15, 15 twists per inch.

We might select a 15-degree angle for the weft, which needs to be soft for filling. Our table gives 11.72 as the figure to divide into 80, and so we arrive at a figure of 7 TPI for our weft.

A quantity sufficient for an experimental warp would be spun at 15 TPI, and sufficient yarn for the required amount of weft spun at 7 TPI. The yarn would, in the early stage of spinning, be compared with commercially available yarns used for similar purposes and, if not wildly dissimilar, the bulk would be spun and woven, with great attention being paid to the way in which they stood up to the loom abrasion and shuttle drag.

The important thing to remember is that up till now *you had no idea*

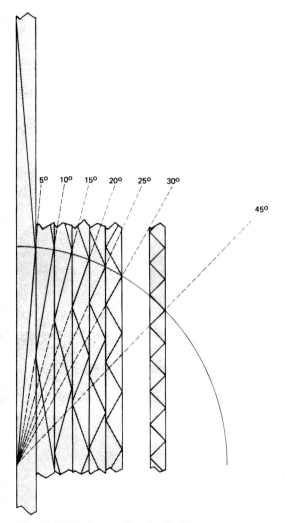

5° 10° 15° 20° 25° 30°

45°

Fig. 116   Various angles of twist in yarns.

at all how much twist was required in the warp and weft. Now, at least you have some guidance. However, there are so many factors which control yarn quality that it would be somewhat surprising if you found the correct combination of yarn diameter and twist angle for the fibre you are using at the first attempt.

143

For instance, the bulk of my yarns are spun 2s worsted (or $\frac{1}{30}$-inch diameter approx.) for plied knitting yarns. With the fibre I use, a medium (fineness scale) 5–6-inch staple Devon Closewool similar to B.W.M.B. specification No. 380, six turns of twist per inch gives what I call a medium twist, producing when plied 6 TPI reverse twist, a soft but durable yarn.

If we reverse the formula we can use the known diameter and TPI to tell us the twist angle. The formula then becomes $\dfrac{\text{diameter}}{\pi \times \text{TPI}} = $ cotangent of twist angle, which in the case under discussion produces $\dfrac{30}{3 \cdot 1416 \times 6} = 1 \cdot 595$, the cotangent of a twist angle of approx. 33 degrees (1·5399), which is given in our guide as a 'hard twist'! The lowest, barely usable, twist at 2s worsted with that fibre I find to be 3 TPI (equal to approx. 17 degrees), and that I would call a very soft twist.

But on the rare occasions when I require warp threads I find that with the same fibre the formula gives a very close result. I spin 12s worsted ($\frac{1}{70}$-inch diameter) using a 30-degree twist angle and find that the description 'hard twist' is just about right. $70 \div 5 \cdot 44 = 12 \cdot 8$ TPI. So I spin 12 TPI.

It will therefore be necessary to carry out accurate tests with the fibre you use before you can allocate yarn characteristics to the various twist angles related to yarn diameters when used with that particular fibre. Variations are bound to occur according to the fineness of the fibre and its staple length. The important thing is to become aware of how necessary it is to know the twist content of your yarns, and how to determine rapidly the amount of twist you are likely to need.

My own experience is that for the larger diameter knitting wools of between $\frac{1}{20}$–$\frac{1}{30}$-inch diameter, 4 TPI produces what I would call a soft twist, 6 TPI a medium, 8 TPI a hard medium and 10 TPI a hard twist, and that twist angles below about 17 degrees are very difficult to produce on a Saxony Wheel in yarns of more than $\frac{1}{40}$-inch diameter.

What seems to have happened when a hand-spinner intended to make a yarn for a particular end use is that she searched around until she found a commercial yarn of the correct diameter and general characteristics required and then she sat down and practised until one similar in size and feel had been produced. The diameter is fairly easy to gauge, it being relatively simple to judge a yarn size by eye—in fact it is part of the hand-spinner's stock-in-trade to do so. But the twist is not so easy to estimate and more often than not she overdid it.

In any case, we must remember that because the commercial spinner produces a yarn that is going to be used (or abused) for a variety of cloth constructions, and that for a great many of them his yarn will be something of a compromise, the hand-spinner may not be copying a yarn that is absolutely ideal for her purposes.

You, on the other hand, now have the opportunity, the ability, to engineer a yarn for your particular end use. You should, with practice, produce yarns and woven and knitted goods which are quite exclusive to you and, because their components have been designed with a particular end use in mind, of quite exceptional quality.

Of the earliest references which I have been able to discover which refer to the twist content of yarns, one is from the book by William Partridge. On page 51 he says:

> 'The filling for broadcloth should have just as much and no more twist than will enable it to draw off the bobbins and follow the shuttle without breakage. It must not only be looser spun, but must also be coarser than the warp.'

The other is contained in J. Lawson's *Progress in Pudsey* and appears in an appendix to a reprint of Baines's *Account of the Woollen Manufacture of England*. Lawson states (page 173):

> 'At first all yarns were spun into coppings, the weft about half the twist of the warp, and the former still wound on to bobbins on the one spindled wheel ready for the weaver's shuttle.'

Chapter 9

A Standard Measure

So far we have only discussed singles yarns as yarns, not as yarns conforming to any particular standard, apart from having a twist content related to their diameter and proposed end use.

The standard against which yarns are equated is the count system. In essence, this relates to the length of yarn which can be spun from 1 lb of fibre. Obviously a yarn of large diameter will take more fibre, and therefore produce less length than a yarn of small diameter.

At first sight the system may appear complicated because instead of making it purely a question of length divided into weight, the yarn is first reeled into hanks of known length and the hanks themselves weighed. The number of hanks which go to make 1 lb will determine the position that that particular yarn takes in the scale of yarn size.

The standard measure for worsted yarns is the number of hanks of 560 yards that together weigh 1 lb.

If we were to spin 1 lb of fibre and found that, when reeled, it measured 560 yards, that yarn would have a count of 1 worsted (or a worsted count of 1, or 1s worsted). Supposing the next yarn we spun was so much finer that, when reeled, it was found to make 4 hanks each of 560 yards to the pound, then that yarn would have a count of 4s worsted. We can say, then, that at 4s worsted, 1 lb of fibre will draw out to 4 times 560 yards, or 2,240 yards (1·2 miles). If we were really ambitious and managed to reel off 22 hanks each of 560 yards from 1 lb of fibre (22s worsted), the yarn would be 22 times 560 = 12,320 yards, or exactly 7 miles to the pound!

It is now essential to state that, although at first sight it might appear that yarns of identical diameter would be indicated whether we say that the yarn equals 22 hanks to the pound or that 1 lb of fibre was spun into 22 hanks, this is not necessarily the case.

For we have not stated the condition of the fibre. Is it greasy? Or scoured? Or scoured and oiled ready for spinning? In each of these three states the quantity of fibre that made up 1 lb would vary. So, therefore, would the length of yarn able to be spun from it.

If, on the other hand, we state that the count is derived from the number of hanks of *yarn*, then since the fibre will always have been subjected to the same pre-spinning treatment, yarns of a given count will always be identical.

Of course, it is not necessary to reel off into hanks of 560 yards all the yarn you have spun before you can work out the count. Say we are spinning a yarn and wish to find its count quickly. We would spin enough to reel off, say, 140 yards, or one-quarter of a hank. (You can do less, of course, but until a fair degree of uniformity in spinning has been reached, the longer length will provide a better average.)

Fig. 118   A simple gear train made of wooden pegs. It has been in constant use now for ten years without giving any trouble.

Fig. 117   This yarn reel, or skeiner, is a copy of one in the Belfast Museum in Northern Ireland. It measures 72 in (1.8 m) in circumference and has two dials, one to record each revolution, or lap, of 2 yards (1.8 m), and the other each 10 revolutions, or 20 yards (18 m).

147

Before the yarn is removed from the skeiner it must be tied at frequent intervals or it will snarl up. For a 6-armed skeiner we would use a minimum of twelve ties, so these would first be cut and weighed. The yarn would now be reeled, tied and weighed; deducting the weight of the ties would reveal the true weight of the yarn. If the true weight of the yarn is multiplied by 4 and the result divided into 1 lb, then the quotient will be the count of that particular yarn (Figs 119, 120 and 121).

Fig. 119 The yarn is reeled direct from the bobbin, passing first under a tension bar. On the right can be seen the twelve ties, carefully weighed.

Fig. 120 Tie the hank at frequent intervals to prevent its tangling when the tension is removed—a minimum of 12 ties on a 6-armed skeiner, 18 for a warp thread.

Fig. 121 The measured yarn and ties are weighed; the product less the tie weight, when divided into 1 lb (454 g), will give the count.

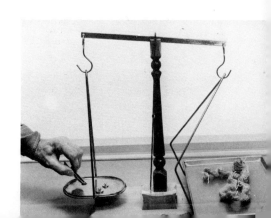

We are now able to state two specifications by which we can convey information about our yarns. We can say what count they are, which will give information about their diameter, and we can give their twist content, which will provide information about their strength and end use suitability. But is it necessary for the hand-spinner or weaver to know such details about the yarns she makes and uses? Well, since I do not suppose that one in a thousand do, it might appear at first sight that it is not. Let us pause to consider that not one hand-spinner in a thousand has previously understood how to determine the amount of twist that a yarn requires—and yet we have already seen how vitally important that aspect is to our trade.

Yarn counts become important when a hand-spinner desires to make goods or produce yarns which conform to known standards. The spinner may wish, for instance, to purchase a warp and use it with hand-spun weft of identical diameter, but lower twist angle.

Let us imagine that a fabric is to be made from a warp with a setting of 30. If the spinner has not supplied the count of the yarn, then this will have first to be worked out. Perhaps the simplest way would be to reel off a measured length of the yarn, say 280 yards or half of a standard worsted hank; if it was found that it weighed 25 g, this would equal 50 g (1¾ oz) for a hank of 560 yards. If we now divide the weight of the hank into 1 lb (453·6 g) the quotient will be the count—453 ÷ 50 = 9 (16 ÷ 1·75 = 9) 9s worsted. So your weft thread will be spun to 9s worsted.

In Appendix III will be found a table giving very close approximations of the diameters expected for yarns in all the worsted counts between 4 and 30. It will be seen that a yarn spun to 9s worsted will have a diameter of $\frac{1}{61}$ inch, which agrees very favourably with the loom setting, i.e. a loom setting of 30 would, for a square fabric, require a yarn of $\frac{1}{60}$-inch diameter. As a cross-check we can wind a length of yarn on our piece of card which measures exactly 1 inch between flanges. If that holds 60 turns = to a yarn of $\frac{1}{60}$-inch diameter, then we can be pretty confident that if we spin a 9s worsted we shall not be very far out.

Let us say we will use a twist angle of 20 degrees, equal to a medium twist, which would be suitable for a weft yarn. Then since:

$$\frac{\text{Diameter of yarn as a whole number}}{\pi \times \text{cotangent of longitudinal angle}} = \text{TPI}$$

$$\frac{60}{3 \cdot 1416 \times 2 \cdot 7475} = \frac{60}{8 \cdot 6315} = 6 \cdot 95 \text{ or 7 twists per inch,}$$

149

we know that we have to spin a yarn to 9s worsted ($\frac{1}{60}$-inch diameter) at 7 TPI.

The 7 TPI is relatively easy—if the ratio of your wheel is 7:1, you have no problem. If 10:1, we divide 10 by 7 = 1·428. So if we draft 1·4 inches of fibre at each pump of the treadle, our yarn will contain 7 TPI. You might in fact be better able to judge 1·5 inches (1$\frac{1}{2}$ inches), in which case the yarn would contain 6·6 TPI, a variation which would probably be acceptable. A 12 to 1 ratio would result in 12÷7 = 1·7, so 1·7 inches at each pump of the treadle would give the required twist. Again, you might be better able to judge 1·75 inches, which would work out at 6·85 TPI, well within our tolerance range.

We can take this reasoning one stage further and say that, if our comfortable spinning rate is one pump a second, equal to 60 revolutions a minute, and if we are making 1·75 inches of yarn per pump, then $1·75 \times 60 \times 60 =$ one hour's production.

$$1·75 \times 60 = 105 \text{ in/min}$$
$$105 \text{ in/min} \times 60 \times 6,300 \text{ in/hour}$$
$$6,300 \text{ inches} = 175 \text{ yards an hour,}$$

which would give you a very good idea of the length of time it would take to complete a given length of (in this case) weft.

To get back to our standard measure and its use as a quality check, we have the commercial yarn by our side as a physical and visual guide to the diameter we have to spin. We know the length of fibre we have to draft at each pump of the treadle, but some experiment will be required until the quantity that will give us our required diameter is found. After we have settled down to a steady diameter which appears fairly close to that of the yarn we wish to duplicate, we might, as a rough check, stop spinning and wind the yarn on our 1-inch (2·5 cm) long card tester. If we get 60–61 turns or laps we can be very self-satisfied, but if more or less, we will have to make the necessary adjustments to the amount of fibre we are drafting and make another test later on, when we have again settled down to a steady rhythm of yarn production.

At the same time as testing the diameter, we would assess the yarn for strength. Remember, the formula is intended to give you a guide, not an exact figure. although once you have a personal factor worked out for it, it will do so. However, now we test the yarn for strength and make allowances in case we need more or less twist—more would require a smaller draft, less a longer draft, of course.

150

Let us say that our rough test shows that we have got it right, $\frac{1}{60}$-inch diameter. We now want to run a proper test, a more accurate test on the yarn. We already know our production rate is 175 yards an hour. We know that $\frac{1}{4}$ hank = 140 yards (560÷4), therefore if we divide 175 yards by 60 we get our production time in yards/min = 2·916, and if we divide our $\frac{1}{4}$ hank by 2·916 = 48, we will know that after, say, 50 minutes' spinning we can expect to be within striking distance of the length of yarn we require. So, after cutting off and weighing a dozen ties, we reel off the yarn, tie it, weight it, subtract the weight of the ties, and if the remainder is 12·5 g, we are to be congratulated indeed. (If $\frac{1}{4}$ hank = 12·5 g, 1 hank will = 50 g, 453·6÷50 = 9; therefore our $\frac{1}{4}$ hank at 12·5 g is the equivalent of 9s worsted.)

We also know that if our production rate is 2.9 yards a minute, we can estimate that in 3 hours 15 minutes we should have spun a hank. So we spin for, say, 3 hours 30 minutes and then reel off the yarn, cut ties, weigh them, and weigh the yarn. If, after subtracting the weight of the ties, the remainder is 50 g (50 into 453·6 = 9 or 9s worsted), then you will have a confidence in your ability *and* your product that you have never known before, because now it will conform to an internationally recognized and assessable standard—one which, given the same information on staple, TPI and count, should be repeatable by a similarly qualified spinner, anywhere in the world.

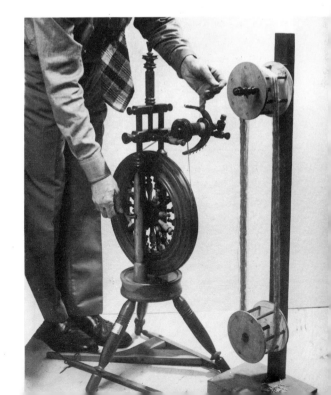

Fig. 122 Re-winding. If the yarn was required to end up on a bobbin for plying or warping, use your wheel as a re-wind machine. You will find you have far greater control if you unhook the treadle and turn the crank by hand—place both loops of the drive band over the bobbin pulley, then the flyer will not revolve.

Although the count system we have been discussing is the international standard used by the hand textile trade, it has in industry been superseded by the *Tex* system.

The Tex system was developed by the International Organization for Standardization (I.S.O.) for describing the linear density of textile yarns and is based on the weight, in grams, of 1 km of yarn. If, therefore, 1 km of yarn weighs 110 g, it would equal 110 Tex.

Like most metrication, it is very simple and direct. To convert the worsted count system we have been discussing to Tex, you divide 885·8 by the worsted count in question. Thus, to convert a worsted count of 8 to Tex: $\dfrac{885 \cdot 8}{8} = 110$ Tex; therefore 110 Tex = 8s worsted. A yarn spun to 8s worsted will be a yarn with a weight of 110 g/km.

Chapter 10
A Miscellany
Plied Yarns, Spinning Tension, Setting the Twist, and Worsted Yarns on the Big Wheel

Plied Yarns

The product of our spinning-wheel is a yarn, a 'singles' yarn of specified quality. It can be used in its singles state for weaving and knitting, or it can be folded or twisted together with other singles yarns to form a different type of yarn—one with a ribbed surface. Yarns so twisted together are described by enumerating the yarns involved, thus 1-ply, 2-ply, 3-ply, etc. Two or more plied yarns twisted together are usually called 'cabled' yarns in the U.K.

The doubling, or plying, can be performed in two ways. The yarns can either be united by twisting them together with the spindle rotating in the same direction as the twist already in the singles yarn, in which case additional twist is added (the fibre angle is increased) and the resultant yarn is very strong, but hard and difficult to control except under tension. Alternatively, the yarns can be twisted together with the spindle rotating in the opposite direction (in which case the fibre angle decreases), resulting in a soft, stable yarn of perhaps less strength, but suitable for a wider range of end uses. It is a relaxed yarn, inert, and will not tangle; consequently it is very easy to manipulate.

Before embarking on the production of fabrics requiring plied yarns, the spinner should consider the amount of extra labour involved over making a singles yarn of the same count. In the first place, two yarns of approximately half the diameter of the singles have to be spun, and here one should remember that spinning time increases as the diameter of the yarn decreases, and then the two yarns have to be combined in a third twisting operation. A plied yarn is therefore very costly, in terms of time, to produce.

What, then, are the advantages to be expected from doubling the yarn? Foremost, perhaps, is the increase in strength and uniformity over a singles yarn of similar count. This is because, no matter how experienced a spinner you are, there are almost certain to be some slight variations in the yarn you have produced. Doubling tends to balance the yarns—the odds against two thin places (should there be any) meeting at the point at which they are plied are long. Doubled yarns can therefore be expected to be more uniformly strong than a singles yarn of similar count.

Their surface texture makes them particularly suitable for many special end uses, and because one method of combining the yarns removes some of the twist it makes them particularly suitable for soft knitting yarns.

Plied or cabled yarns of different colours are frequently used to produce interesting colour blends.

There is just as much need for careful and accurate control in plying as there is in spinning, and very much the same action is called for. It is much easier to ply from yarns contained on bobbins than from yarn which is balled, so a liberal supply of bobbins is necessary. (The trouble with balls arises when they are nearly run out, for then they tend to rise rather than unwind. The problem can be overcome by placing the balls inside a box with holes pierced in the lid, through which the yarns emerge.) It must be remembered that the singles yarn straight from the wheel will tend to snarl up when tension is relaxed, and this can be a curse, especially if the bobbins are in a vertical rack down by the spinner's feet, for two yarns in such close proximity may tend to tangle and interrupt the smooth flow of either or both yarns to the spinner's fingers.

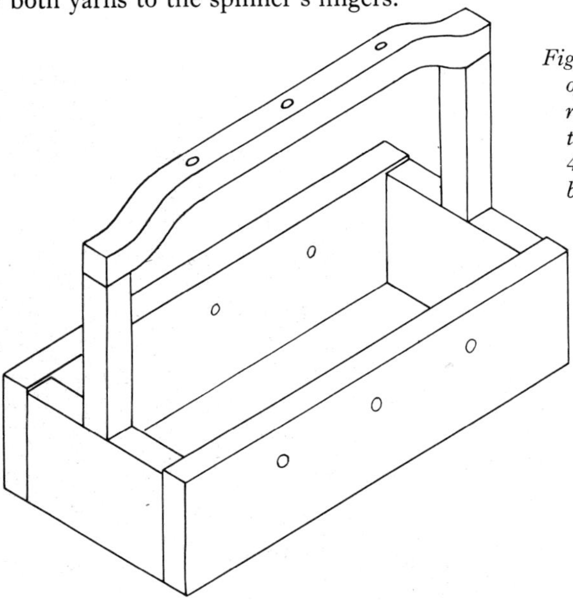

Fig. 123 Drawing of the bobbin rack to take three standard 4-in (102-mm) bobbins.

154

Figures 123 and 124 show a three-bobbin rack which I designed to obviate this problem. The handle is bored above each bobbin; the yarns, passing through the handle, are held well away from each other as they progress towards the spindle. The dimensions are fairly critical; do not be tempted to reduce the distance between the handle and the base, for plenty of room must be allowed for the yarn to unwind from either side, or flange end, of the bobbin. If the handle is too close, the angle at which the yarn passes through the guide hole from the extreme edge of the bobbin is so great that drag on the yarn becomes excessive.

Fig. 124   A plying rack designed to keep the yarns apart and so avoid tangles between the yarn supply and R.H.

Material	*Pine, or timber of choice, perhaps chosen to match that of spinning-wheel.*
Sides	*Two off; $12 \times 3 \times \frac{3}{4}$ in ($300 \times 75 \times 20$ mm).*
Ends	*Two off; $4\frac{1}{2} \times 3 \times \frac{3}{4}$ in ($110 \times 75 \times 20$ mm)*
Handle Supports	*Two off; $5 \times \frac{3}{4} \times \frac{3}{4}$ in ($130 \times 20 \times 20$ mm).*
Handle (Curved)	*One off; $12 \times 1\frac{5}{8} \times \frac{3}{4}$ in ($300 \times 42 \times 20$ mm).*
or	
Handle (Straight)	*One off; $12 \times \frac{3}{4} \times \frac{3}{4}$ in ($300 \times 20 \times 20$ mm)*

The curved handle is not essential, nor are the turned supports, but you are going to look at it, use it, for a long time, so you might as well take that little extra trouble now, which can pay such enormous pleasure dividends over the years.

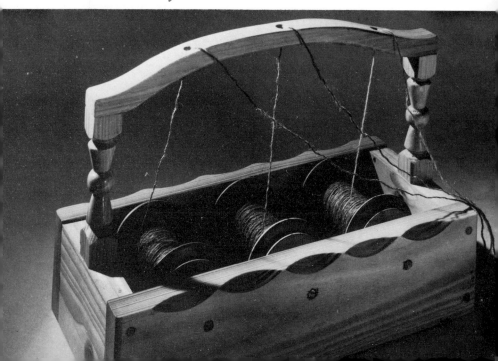

By far the greater bulk of doubled yarns are made with the direction of twist opposing that which was imparted when the yarn was made—the inherent twist, we will call it. If the yarn was made with the wheel rotating in a clockwise direction (a 'Z' twist), then for plying the wheel would be rotated in an anti-clockwise direction, to produce an 'S' twist.

In all the books I have read on hand-spinning, the operating instructions for plying are the same—take the ends of the yarns to be plied, join them together, pass them through the spindle on to the bobbin, hold or guide the yarn through the fingers and start the wheel rotating in the reverse direction. As the yarns wind on, so they will twist together. Well, they do, after a fashion—but my experience with that method is that the resulting ply is very uneven, depending solely on how freely the bobbins run. Some lengths have a tight spiral, others a long, loose one, not at all like the uniform yarns we purchase. Sometimes, too, one yarn will drag and the other wind about it like the flow of steps in a spiral staircase but not at all like the ribbing we expect in a plied yarn. In this method no account at all is taken of the twist that went into the singles, or the effect of the reverse twist that unites them, both of which must influence the finished yarn.

My own preference (for knitting yarns) is to ply with the same amount of reverse twist as that which was used to make the singles. Therefore, if the singles yarns were spun at 7 TPI, then the plying would be done in the reverse direction at 7 TPI. Since the combined twist of the two singles is $7 \times 2 = 14$, minus 7 TPI plying twist, the finished yarn will be composed of two yarns with a combined twist of 7 TPI, which will make the yarn very soft, ideally suitable for knitting. However, a woven structure may require a stronger, and therefore a more tightly-twisted yarn, and so it may be necessary to start with a singles having a greater than normal twist angle, so that when the reverse twist has been deducted, the yarn has the handle and strength for its anticipated end use.

It must be obvious that there are several choices open to the yarn designer:

1   Yarns of equal count and TPI can be plied with the same, but reverse, twist;

2   Yarns of equal count and TPI can be plied with a reverse twist either in excess of, or less than, the inherent twist;

3   Yarns of unequal count and/or TPI can be plied with reverse twist unrelated to either component.

4 1, 2 and 3 can be duplicated with twist which complements the inherent twist.

If, then, we accept that the control of twist in plying is just as important as the control of twist in spinning, it is obvious that the old and oft-advocated method of letting the yarns ply themselves in a free and easy manner will not be good enough for us.

In fact, we require a very similar hand action and twist control to that used in spinning.

Having placed two bobbins on the plying-rack and passed the yarns up through the guide holes, we join them (tie them) on to a length of yarn which is attached to the bobbin and emerges through the spindle. Adjust the tension to that which you have grown accustomed for spinning, turn the bobbin in an anti-clockwise direction until the knot of the join is through the last of the flyer hooks, and turn the wheel until the crank is at 10 o'clock.

The DH performs a very similar function as when spinning, except that it is now used to position the yarns at the point of twisting, as well as to draft them. The second finger is used to space the yarns, one passing on either side of it. The index finger and thumb are positioned close in front of the second finger and grip the two yarns between them for drafting. At the end of the drafting stroke the DH returns, or slides down the yarn, to its original position, closely followed by the twist, which unites the two yarns with a completely even rib. With practice, the actual uniting of the yarns can be made to take place in front of the second finger, an ideal position, for then the yarns are plied in absolutely even quantities, producing a beautifully even rib. If the draft is a constant and the twist is a constant, then the ply will be quite professionally uniform (Fig. 125).

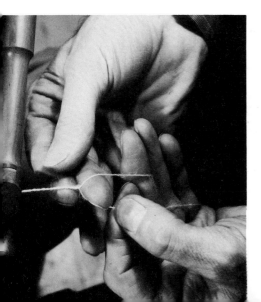

Fig. 125 The D.H. fingers opened to show the point of ply right in front of the second finger.

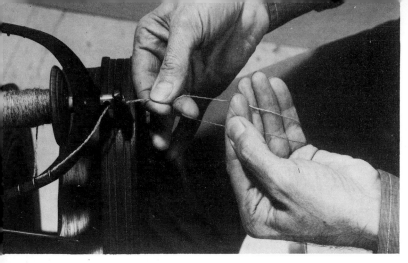

*Fig. 126   The yarns pass either side of the second finger
and are drafted by the index finger and
thumb; tension is applied in the drafting
zone by passing one yarn between the R.H.
index finger and thumb, the other between
the index and the second fingers.*

The RH is used to prevent the yarns becoming tangled, and to ensure a constant and freely-moving supply of yarn to the DH. One yarn is tensioned between finger and thumb, the other between second and third finger (Fig. 126).

The plying draft will control and determine the ribbing on the yarn. A longer draft for a given amount of twist will produce a more widely-spaced rib than a short draft. But remember that it will also affect the amount of residual twist in the yarn. The final yarn, then, is very much a designed product.

Let us imagine that we have been attracted by a certain yarn and wish to produce one similar in appearance. First of all, we would have to count the number of ribs to the inch—let us say that there are eight. This, then, indicates a reverse ply of 4 TPI, since each twist will produce two ribs, one for each yarn. The yarn we require must be soft for knitting—from previous experience we know that a residual twist of 6 TPI gives us just the handle, the spring, the softness we require. Two-fold yarns with a residual twist of 6 TPI $=$ 3 TPI per yarn; 3 TPI plus the two per yarn that will be removed in the reverse twist would indicate that we must start with singles yarn with a twist of 5 TPI. So we work out the count and spin the required quantity at 5 TPI. We ply them at 4 revolutions of the spindle with a 1-inch draft, or divide the spindle revolutions by 4 to indicate the draft, and that should produce a yarn with the surface characteristics we admired (8 ribs per inch) with the softness and handle we associate with 6 TPI (5×2 = 10. 10−4 = 6).

We can now be a little more accurate in describing our plied yarn, for instead of calling it simply a 2-ply—which really only tells you that 2 singles yarns have been twisted together, we can give a far better impression by detailing the count of the singles. Thus, 2 singles 20s worsted would, when plied, give a yarn described as 2/20s. A cloth construction could be given as 2/20s warp, 10s singles for weft. You would then know you had to spin sufficient 20s count to supply the warp after the yarns had been doubled (producing 2/20s), and sufficient yarn spun 10s for the singles weft.

It is very much an area for experiment. The possible combinations are vast, though time-consuming. Once again, I must emphasize the importance of entering everything you do in a work book. The various quantities of fibre, staple, colour, twist, count, ply, each of which can exercise an important influence on our finished yarns, are now far too great to be contained accurately in one's memory. It is a great waste of time ever to have to repeat an experiment because you were too slip-shod (or excited) to make notes at the time.

It is perhaps worth reminding ourselves that the sheen present on most worsted yarns is caused by the light being able to reflect from the edges of the fibres as they lie side by side in the yarn. The sheen is nearly always noticeable, except when very coarse and hairy fibres are spun. It is similar to the effect obtained when special lustre fibres are spun, though not nearly so intense.

The effect of decreasing the fibre angle is to present the fibre with its length more nearly in line with the axis of the yarn. Hence, singles yarns twisted 'Z' and doubled 'S' will exhibit a greater degree of sheen than when plied 'Z', because the increased twist caused by plying in the same direction as the inherent twist increases the fibre angle and forces it more and more at right-angles to the yarn axis (Fig. 127).

Fig. 127(a) Yarn spun 'Z', plied 'S';

Fig. 127(b) Yarn spun 'Z' and plied 'Z'.

159

Tension

When we first started to use the spinning-wheel, we set the tension so that the yarn being twisted would wind on freely. Quite a low tension will create a strong pull on the yarn when the bobbin is empty, but as the bobbin fills, the point at which the yarn wraps around the bobbin moves progressively out towards the rim of the bobbin flanges.

The further out from the bobbin core that the yarn contact is made, the greater the braking action that the yarn will exert on the rotation of the bobbin. Eventually, a stage can be reached when the braking action is greater than the traction of the drive band, and the yarn wind-on slows down or may cease altogether, with the result that the yarn receives more than its specified amount of twist.

The answer is simple—gently increase the tension on the drive band until the yarn tugs at your fingers with just about the same degree of pull as when the bobbin was empty. It might be necessary to make such an adjustment to the tension three or four times whilst filling a bobbin. Since the amount of tension required is in direct ratio to the bobbin core diameter, it becomes a matter of some importance that the yarn is evenly distributed over the whole area of the bobbin. Frequent stops to change the yarn from one flyer hook to the next are therefore necessary. One adjustment of tension will then be right for a gradual increase in core diameter over the whole area of the core between the bobbin flanges. You should make a point of becoming aware of tension, or the lack of it. Do not wait until the yarn fails to wind-on before making the necessary adjustment.

You will find that an even distribution of yarn over the core will make unreeling the bobbin a simpler task. The problem here is that as the yarn is removed, the core diameter reduces in size and the rotation of the bobbin increases. If the build-up of yarn in spinning was haphazard, with sudden variations in core diameter taking place, the momentum imparted can cause the bobbin either to overrun badly, resulting in the yarn's tangling up, or it can cause a sudden braking effect which, on fine yarns, can cause the yarn to snap. An even build-up will lead to a steady increase in the bobbin rotation as the yarn is removed without there being any danger of the yarn's being damaged.

It is particularly important when several bobbins are being unwound simultaneously, as in creeling or plying.

The spinner may sometimes notice that when the bobbin is empty the pull on the yarn spun in the early stage is quite considerable and that the effort required to prevent the yarn's parting at the drafting zone and disappearing into the spindle eye causes the DH finger and thumb to be pinched quite tightly over the yarn.

As the bobbin fills, the pull on the yarn becomes less and the ache in the DH digits eases. If, however, the yarn spun at the higher tension was examined it would probably be found to be smoother than that spun at the lower tension, although the twist imparted was identical.

I think the reason is twofold. The increased tension leads to increased pressure of the DH finger and thumb, pressure at just the point where the twist coiled the parallel fibres into a yarn, and this seems to tuck all the fibre ends into the yarn more effectively, making it quite smooth. The other reason is probably that the higher tension prevents the yarn relaxing and holds the contour to its freshly spun state. The higher tension will also enable more yarn to be wound on the bobbin, although I doubt if that is a really important consideration.

So, although we started by saying 'apply enough tension to provide optimum wind-on conditions and no more' it can be shown that an increase in tension can have an effect in improving your yarns. It is something you should grow into gradually, as the muscles of the DH finger and thumb grow accustomed to their task over a period of several months. To rush it will cause unbearable aches.

I have found that the smoothness of the yarn, and therefore its threadiness, can be enhanced if, combined with the slightly higher tension, a modified DH position is adopted (Fig. 128).

Fig. 128   You can see by the way that the yarn presses into the flesh of the index finger that some considerable tension is present—you can also see what a very smooth yarn it produces.

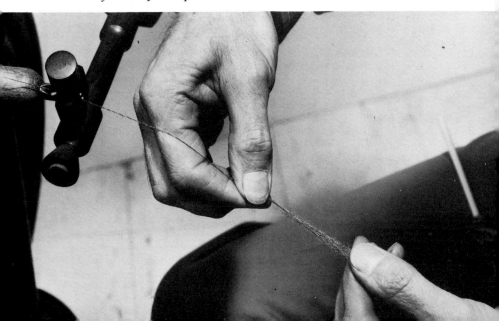

If the angle of the hand relative to the spindle is altered, so that the yarn, after leaving the twisting point between the finger and thumb of the DH, has the maximum amount of contact with the skin of the hand, any stray fibres that have escaped the contours of the yarn will be smoothed into place when the yarn surface rotates as the twist passes down it into the freshly drafted fibre.

With care, the yarn can be made to have contact with just about the whole of the index finger.

The effectiveness is more noticeable when using a short staple fibre than when using long, of course, and it is not such a naturally comfortable position in which to hold the hand; but it does produce a very smooth yarn indeed.

I hesitated whether to include this or not, because it is something that should be grown into, for it means that the drafting platform can no longer be seen and the drafting fingers are therefore unable to perform their task. It is an advanced technique. Perfect the other first, and try it only when normal drafting is an easy and effortless task.

The time to attempt this new method is when, through practice, the quality of your rovings has improved to the extent that the fingers of the drafting platform are being used less and less frequently to control errant strands, and eventually only as a background to the fibre.

Setting the Twist

If the end tension is removed from freshly-spun yarn it will tend to unwind itself because of the natural springiness of the fibre. This causes the yarn to coil or snarl about itself to the extent that sometimes the yarn is impossible to unravel. The greater the twist angle, the greater the problem is likely to be, and yet we must empty the bobbin to enable us to carry on spinning.

The way you tackle the problem will depend on your scale of operations and on the type of yarn you are producing; it is a problem almost exclusively associated with singles yarns or plied yarns which have been twisted in the same direction as the singles which form them. Plied or cabled weaving yarns made contra to the spinning twist rarely suffer from it, and when they do the treatment is the same as for singles. Plied knitting yarns should never be affected—they should never be that tightly twisted.

You will have noticed that yarn forgotten and left on a bobbin for weeks does not show this tendency to snarl up. The fibres, you might say, have become set in their new shape as a yarn. Since we cannot wait weeks for this to happen naturally, we must hasten things along artificially. The usual method is to remove the yarn from the bobbin and to skein it, either on the yardage counter or on a floor swift. It can now be tied with a loop of string every 3 or 4 inches (8–10 cm), removed from the skeiner, and either hung up under tension—just enough to stretch the yarn out and keep it straight, something in the order of 1 kg (35·27 oz) to a 100 g (3½ oz) skein of 8s worsted would be about right. You can, of course, leave the yarn on the swift or skeiner and adjust the tension to the maximum, but it is doubtful whether the yarn would be sufficiently set by the time that the next bobbin was ready for unloading.

If the yarn is scoured to remove the spinning oil before it is woven or knitted and put under tension while it is drying, it will be found to be quite stable by the time it is ready for use. The larger the area of the tensioning appliance the better, because the skein can be more evenly spread, with the increased likelihood that each thread will bear a similar weight. The tensioners illustrated were made several years ago and proved to be very satisfactory. A side benefit of the larger area is that the yarn dries that much more quickly (Fig. 129).

Fig. 129 With rollers and weight 15 in (380 mm) wide by 4 in (102 mm) diameter there is ample room, and weight, for a bobbin full of yarn.

It is rare indeed for a spinner to have enough bobbins for her spinning-wheel to enable her to spin all the yarn for a warp and to place the bobbins on the creel as she fills them. This would appear to be a sound answer, because then the yarn would set while it was waiting for the remainder to be spun. If warping were delayed for a few days after the final bobbin were filled, little trouble would be experienced—the time could be occupied by spinning weft, perhaps.

Although I have never come across a hand-weaver who passes the yarn through a vat of size before beaming, the process would certainly set the yarn.

The size, a glutinous substance, holds the fibres of a yarn in place and helps to avoid the fraying of the warp caused by the motion of the heddles. Sizing is always mentioned in books written for the commercial weaver, although omitted by Luther Hooper and Elsie Davenport.

I think that, were I a weaver, I would size up some experimental warps and assess the results. A quite simple set-up could be arranged whereby the yarn passed from a bobbin to a tensioner, down into the size vat, under a roller and up on to a warping board or a warp-run where the yarn could dry without actually touching.

Yarns can be sized in the skein but must be opened out to dry or they will tend to adhere to each other as they dry. It seems to be as good a way as any to set the yarn, and might well improve your fabrics into the bargain, for surely the process would have been omitted in industry were it possible to do so. After all, the dampening of weft (filling) was discontinued a hundred years ago, but sizing is still a commercial undertaking. You may care to experiment with the size formulae contained in Appendix IV.

Worsted Spinning on the Big Wheel

There is really only one problem associated with spinning worsted yarns on a Big Wheel, and that is how to hold the roving. You will see how I overcame the problem in Fig. 130. It works very well, with the roving right where it is wanted, by the side of the RH, yet not in the way at all. Some shirt cuffs are tight enough to hold the spindle securely, while others will not. A crepe bandage works very well and is useful in the summer when, perhaps, one wants one's sleeves rolled up.

The drafting action is rather different when using the Big Wheel, because the amount of twist in the embryonic yarn between the spindle point and the DH is only sufficient to hold the fibres together. The TPI

Fig. 130 Method of holding roving spindle when using the Big Wheel.

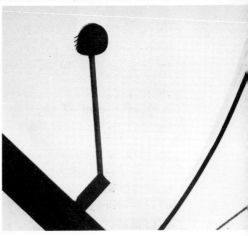

Fig. 131 A 1-in (2.5-cm) diameter ball of oak taps against the rim at each revolution while drafting, but centrifugal force holds it against the rim when the wheel is speeded up for the final twist insertion.

required to do this will depend on the staple and the quantity of fibre being drafted, but once a figure has been arrived at it can be maintained with absolute regularity by counting the revolutions of the wheel—something attached to the rim which clicks against the stand at each turn of the wheel is a great help (Fig. 131).

Fig. 132 A 'clicker' is necessary because, during two-handed drafting, the spinner's back is towards the wheel, which will rotate two or three turns from the impetus given by one flick of the wrist—but the number of rotations must be known.

Fig. 133 The yarn pinched by the R.H. and the wheel speeded up to insert the final twist. These photographs were taken with the wheel revolving fast, but the electronic lamps have 'killed' the action. Note the clicker held against the wheel rim.

Because there is no tug of wind-on tension on a Big Wheel, an extremely fine yarn can be spun, and since the amount of drafting twist is so low the DH fingers can leave go of the yarn as they move forward for a fresh pinch of fibre. In fact, very often it is essential that the DH fingers do leave go of the yarn, because with the twist inserted being only just enough to cause the fibres to hold together, some strands would pull out and ruck up if the DH fingers attempted to slide down the yarn with the sort of action we have been accustomed to use on the Saxony Wheel (Fig. 132).

Some very small amount of twist will precede them and involve fibres in the centre of the roving which, when drawn out, do, as James remarks, produce an especially smooth yarn. Once the predetermined length of yarn has been drafted, the yarn is pinched by the RH fingers where it enters the drafting zone, and the wheel rotated by the DH to insert the required amount of extra twist necessary to bring the length of yarn up to the end use specification (Fig. 133).

Say a warp thread of 8s worsted with a 30-degree twist angle was contemplated. From Appendix III we see that it would have an approximate diameter of $\frac{1}{57}$ inch. Appendix II gives us the product of the cotangent of $30° \times \pi$ as 5·441. Therefore:

$$57 \text{ divided by } 5\cdot441 = 10\cdot4$$

Our yarn, then, will require 10 or $10\frac{1}{2}$ TPI. For every turn of my Big Wheel the spindle revolves 40 times. Therefore, if we use a standard draw of 36 inches, the yarn will require 360 turns of twist in it, or 9 turns of the wheel, of which 3 might be used in the actual drafting, the remaining 6 being inserted after drafting has ceased, and the fibre supply pinched to prevent twist entering into it. You will see that if 3 turns = 120 twists are used in drafting (equal to 3·33 TPI) the yarn will be very fragile indeed, and so low will be the inherent twist that there is no danger of its entering the fibre supply and locking the fibres into an undraftable mass.

There is no need to have any tension on the yarn at all between the spindle point and the DH when drafting takes place. The yarn can be quite slack, because, provided it is held at a 15-degree angle or more, it will slip off the spindle point as it rotates.

It is after the prescribed length has been drafted that the tension can be increased to that sufficient to keep the yarn tight. Remember, very fine yarns require more TPI, consequently they tend to snarl up if a steady tension is not maintained after the end use TPI has been inserted. It is especially important to judge the wind-on tension accurately; too much may cause a fine thread to snap, especially when the cop or package is reaching its maximum size, for the wind-on speed will vary very considerably from empty spindle to full cop—but a couple of days' spinning will teach you how much tension to use.

There is no bobbin on a Big Wheel, and if the yarn is wound directly on to the spindle it has to be unwound and transferred to some other support before spinning can re-commence. I find that brown paper wrapped round the spindle a few turns where the yarn will wind on makes a useful core upon which the cop can be formed. It is slipped off the spindle with the yarn when the available space has been used up. Cops formed in this way can be creeled by passing an axle through the hollow centre, which will allow the cop to revolve freely as it unwinds (Figs 134 and 135).

Care must be taken in building up the cop; the method used will depend on the way the cop is unwound. It is possible to unwind the yarn by pulling it off over the point of the spindle, down the spindle axis. As the yarn

Fig. 134 Making a bobbin core by winding a length of brown wrapping paper around the spindle—make sure the wrap goes in the same direction as spinning rotation. If you use a bobbin rack, cut your pieces of paper narrow enough to fit inside!

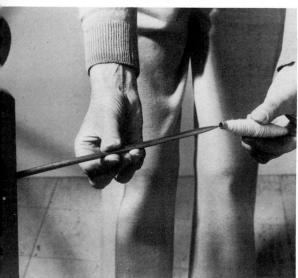

Fig. 135 The core will grip the spindle tight enough to ensure wind-on, but will slip off easily for transfer to plying rack or creel.

unwinds, for each loop that comes off, one turn of twist will be gained. That may not be important when the cop is large, since 6 or more inches (more than 15 cm) may come off per loop, but as the cop decreases in size, so the twist gain is spread over an ever-decreasing length of yarn. Of course, this can be compensated for in spinning, but the variation in twist over the full range from full to empty cop will take some working out!

So I opt for the package that I can slide off the spindle and unwind in the conventional way, like an ordinary bobbin.

For yarn that is unwound along the spindle axis, the cop must be built up so that each wrap of yarn will pull off without dragging off others adjacent to it. The cop is started with a small lump, or bunch, of yarn, about a couple of inches away from the spindle bearing but tapering over, say, 3 inches (8 cm), towards the point. If now each successive wrap of yarn goes from the bunch and back towards the point, once the cop build-up has started, the increase in size is uniform over the whole area, tapering in a cone shape towards the spindle tip. If the yarn is laid on with a criss-cross pattern, it will prevent one layer sinking into and binding to that which is already on the spindle. If, when removing the yarn from the spindle (called 'doffing' in the trade), it is wound on to a skeiner, the action of the yarn pulling off over the point imparts a circular motion to the thread, which causes the yarn to curve outwards from the point where it leaves the cop. If you judge the speed of re-wind just right, the yarn will leave the cop with an angle that will enable it to unwind freely. It also helps to prevent the yarn dragging off adjacent turns near the tip of the cone. Again, it is very much a matter for experiment.

Plying on the Big Wheel is rather more difficult than on a Saxony Wheel. But if spinners will only content themselves with a small draft, they will soon get into the swing of it.

Fig. 136 Two bobbins in the rack, a length of yarn plied and just about to be backed off—tension is rather difficult to maintain.

The main problem is associated with the fact that the yarns on the bobbin draw off as the RH is drawn away from the spindle, and so, when the plied yarn is wound on, the yarns between the RH and the bobbin become difficult to control because they are no longer under tension. The answer then (I find) is to sit down at the wheel and only make short drafts of 12 to 18 inches (30–45 cm), which can be wound on fairly easily and yet maintain some tension on the yarns coming up to the RH from the bobbin rack (Fig. 136).

Similar ply principles apply. The reverse twist will be worked out in exactly the same way—only the method of inserting it and the drafting are different, for here the RH will have to draft the yarns and control the wind-on while the right hand turns the wheel. I have never managed to obtain as even a ply on the Big Wheel as I can on a Saxony machine. We often spin on the Big Wheel and ply the spools on the Saxony.

The Big Wheel is a good example of quality versus quantity, for it can produce worsted yarns of superlative quality, though somewhat slowly when compared with the greater output of the Saxony Wheel. Using it is an absolute pleasure. Here we have a machine that is just about as basic as it is possible to make, and yet it can produce some of the finest yarns in the world, as fine as gossamer or as coarse as a seaman's jersey yarn.

The spinner never has the feeling that her machine is running away with her, as is so often the early experience with the Saxony Wheel. It is a dignified device, a senior citizen of the mechanical hierarchy, and seems often to impart some of its quiet, unhurried efficiency to its user.

Fancy Yarns

Just about every book on hand-spinning I have read devotes considerable space to this aspect of our trade, but it is one that so far I have not had time to explore.

However, now that you have the ability to produce plain yarns to the standard of professional spinning specifications, you should be able to apply the same basic principles to this type of work.

Appendix I
British Wool Fleeces

The range of fleeces set out in the table below have been specially selected by the British Wool Marketing Board* to cover a wide range of hand-spinning requirements.

Type No.	Description	Average Staple Length (inches)	Handle	Colour	Approximate Weight of Normal Greasy Fleece (kilograms)
84209	Fine Wool Clun, etc.	3	Soft	White	2/3
84308	Romney Marsh	4/5	Medium	White	3/4
84323	Halfbreed	6/7	Soft/Medium	White	3/4
84343	Halfbreed (Leicester type)	6/7	Medium	White	3/4
84392	Jacobs	5/6	Soft	Piebald	2/3
84490	Lustre Grey	7/8	Medium/Harsh	Grey	3/4
84523	Lincoln	10/12	Harsh	White lustre	6/7
84603	Cheviot	3/5	Soft	White	2/3
84630	Shetland	1/2	Very soft	White	1
84631	Shetland	1/3	Very soft	Browns	1
84632	Shetland	1/4	Very soft	Grey/black	1
84690	Welsh	3/4	Soft	Grey/black	1/2
84693	Cheviot	3/5	Soft/medium	Grey/black	2/3
84719	Herdwick	3/6	Harsh	Grey/black	1/2

The following table provides a general guide to the use of fleeces.

Staple Length	Recommendation	Qualities	Use
2 in	For the experienced spinner suitable for woollen spinning	Soft to medium	Suitable for spinning apparel fabrics
3–4 in	Recommended for beginners suitable for woollen spinning	Medium to harsh	Suitable for tweeds, coat and upholstery fabrics
5–7 in	Recommended for beginners suitable for worsted spinning	Harsh	Suitable for upholstery and floor coverings
Over 7 in	Better suited to the experienced spinner		

*The British Wool Marketing Board, Kew Bridge House, Kew Bridge, Brentford, Middlesex TW8 OEL, England.

British wool grade specifications (England, Wales and Scotland)

Grade	Degree of fineness (inches)	Length of staple (inches)	Handle of wool	Degree of lustre	Degree of springiness	Colour	Strength	Other factors
331 Deep Halfbred Hog Arable	"	—	"	Slight	"	Poor and soily	Reasonably sound	—
334 Halfbred Hog Cast	Irregular 48/54s	Irregular may be rather short	Fairly soft	Some	"	Probably poor, often yellowish Soily	Variable, possibly weak	Kemp possible
335 Halfbred Hog Cast Light Arable	"	"	"	"	"	Soily	"	Some evidence of cottiness, also kemp possible
338 Halfbred Ewe and Wether	Fine 54/50s	Uniform 5	Reasonably soft	"	High	Good	Very sound	—
339 Halfbred Ewe and Wether No. 2	"	"	"	"	"	Inferior	Fairly sound	—
340 Halfbred Ewe and Wether Light Arable	"	"	"	"	Good	Poor and soily	Sound	—
342 Deep Halfbred Ewe and Wether	Medium 50/48s	" 6	"	"	High	Good	Very sound	—
343 Deep Halfbred Ewe and Wether No. 2	"	Irregular	"	"	Some	Fair	Fairly sound	—
344 Deep Halfbred Ewe and Wether Light Arable	"	"	"	"	"	Poor and soily	"	—
345 Halfbred Ewe and Wether Cast	" 48/54s	Irregular usually short in growth	Fairly soft	"	Usually some	Poor	Variable, often distinct weakness	May have some kempy fibres and cottiness
346 Halfbred Ewe and Wether Cast Light Arable	"	"	"	"	"	Poor and shabby	"	May have some evidence of cottiness or kempy fibres
347 Halfbred Hog, Ewe and Wether Kempy	" 50/54s	Variable	Variable	"	Some	Good	Sound	—
348 Halfbred Cotts	"	May be several variations of other faults but cottiness is the determining factor						
349 Halfbred Hog, Ewe and Wether Kempy Light Arable	"	Variable	Variable	None	Some	Soily	Sound	—
374 Exmoor Horn	Fine/Medium	3–4½	Harsh	None	High	Good	Sound	May show odd grey fibres
375 Exmoor Horn No. 2	"	—	"	"	"	Fair	Fairly sound	"
376 Exmoor Horn Cast	"	3½–5	Harsh but may be variable	"	Some	Poor	May be weak	"

No. & Breed	Fineness	Quality No.	Length of Staple	Length (in.)	Handle	Lustre	Springiness	Colour / Soil	Strength	Grey Fibres
377 Exmoor Horn Light Arable	Fine/Medium	50/54s	—	3–4½	Harsh	None	High	Soily	May be weak	May show odd grey fibres
378 Exmoor Horn Discoloured	"	"	Irregular	"	"	Some slight	"	Discoloured	Sound	Subject to odd grey fibre
379 Light Crossbred	"	50s	—	5–6	Fairly soft	"	Good	Very good	"	May be subject to odd grey fibre
380 Light Crossbred No. 2	Fine/Medium	"	May be variable	"	"	Slight	"	Fairly good	Fairly sound	"
383 Heavy Crossbred	Medium/ Low	48/46s	—	7–8½	Slightly harsh	"	Some	Very good	Sound	"
384 Heavy Crossbred No. 2	"	"	Variable	"	"	"	"	Fairly good	Fairly sound	"
385 Crossbred Cotts	"	"	"	"	"	"	"	"	"	"

May be several variations of other faults but cottiness is the determining factor

Terms used in the above table

Degree of Fineness The diameter of the wool fibre influences to a large extent the use to which the wool can be put and also the length of yarn that can be spun from a given weight of wool. Users and manufacturers normally use a series of "quality numbers" to indicate fibre diameter. These numbers, in ascending order of fineness, are 28s (the thickest, coarsest fibres), 32s, 36s, 40s, 44s, 46s, 48s, 50s, 56s, 58s, 60s, 64s, 66s, 70s, 90s, 100s (the very thinnest, finest fibres). Most British wools are within the range 28s to 58s. Quality numbers are not based on any particular unit of measurement; they are standards handed down from generation to generation of woolmen and can be learned only by practical experience and handling of wools.

Length of Staple This is the measurement of the unstretched staple from tip to base. The figures quoted are the standards for each grade.

Handle of Wool The softness or harshness of the wool when handled.

Degree of Lustre This refers to the amount of gloss or sheen visible on the fibres. Degree of lustre varies greatly between different types. A bright lustre is an asset for certain manufacturing processes.

Degree of Springiness The extent to which a handful of wool will expand again after being compressed and released. Springiness is a valuable quality of most British wools.

Colour The nearness of the wool to white (or black in the case of black fleeces).

Strength The ability of the staple to resist breakage during manufacture. The word "sound" is used to describe wool of satisfactory strength rather than "strong" which, in wool terminology, refers to thick or coarse fibres. The opposite to a sound wool is a "tender" wool. Tender wools may have a break in all the fibres at one point in the staple as a result of illness or drought.

Other terms used include the following

Grey Fibres The presence of grey or black fibres in a fleece restricts its dyeing range to the darker shades. This fault occurs in many of the white-woolled breeds.

Kemp A brittle white fibre, shed during the growth of the fleece, which is extremely difficult to dye. In Welsh wool red kemp is often found.

Light Arable A term applied to wool which contains up to 6% soil or sand due to the sheep having been run on arable crops.

Arable A term applied to wool which contains over 6% of soil or sand.

Hog Refers to wool from a sheep that is first shorn as a yearling.

Ewe and Wether Refers to wool from the second and subsequent shearings.

Yield The amount of clean dry wool remaining after the dirt and grease in the fleece have been scoured away commercially.

Appendix II

Twist Angle (degrees)	Cotangent of Longitudinal Angle (of twist angle)	× 3.1416
5°	11·430	35·908
7°	8·1443	25·586
10°	5·6713	17·816
12°	4·7046	14·779
15°	3·7320	11·724
17°	3·2708	10·275
20°	2·7475	8·631
22°	2·4751	7·775
25°	2·1445	6·737
27°	1·9626	6·165
30°	1·7320	5·441
32°	1·6003	5·027
35°	1·4281	4·486
37°	1·3270	4·168
40°	1·1917	3·743
42°	1·1106	3·489
44°	1·0355	3·253

Appendix III

Worsted Count	Approximate Diameter in Fractions of 1 inch	
	Crossbred Worsted	Botany Worsted
4	1/41	1/44
5	1/45	1/48
6	1/49	1/53
7	1/54	1/57
8	1/57	1/61
9	1/61	1/65
10	1/64	1/69
11	1/67	1/72
12	1/70	1/75
13	1/73	1/79
14	1/76	1/81
15	1/79	1/84
16	1/81	1/87
17	1/84	1/90
18	1/86	1/92
19	1/88	1/94
20	1/91	1/97
21	1/93	1/100
22	1/95	1/102
23	1/98	1/104
24	1/100	1/106
25	1/102	1/109
26	1/104	1/111
27	1/106	1/113
28	1/108	1/115
29	1/110	1/117
30	1/111	1/119

Twists Per Inch = TPI (Twists per 25·4 mm)

To find the draft for any given TPI once the spindle-wheel ratio is known, divide the required TPI into the spindle revolutions.

Example 1: What draft will produce 8 TPI with a 15:1 ratio?

$$\frac{15}{8} = 1·8$$ Thus, if a 1·8-in draft is given for each pump of the treadle, the yarn will receive 8 TPI.

Example 2: What draft will produce 5 TPI with a 12:1 ratio?

$$\frac{12}{5} = 2·4$$ Therefore, a 2·4-in draft will produce a yarn of 5 TPI.

Draft divided into Spindle Revolutions will produce TPI.

Example 1: What TPI will a 1½-in draft produce with an 11:1 spindle ratio?

$$\frac{11}{1 \cdot 5} = 7 \cdot 3, \text{ say 7 TPI.}$$

Example 2: What TPI will a ¾-in draft produce with a 7:1 spindle ratio?

$$\frac{7}{0 \cdot 75} = 9 \cdot 3, \text{ say 9 TPI.}$$

Yarn Diameter

Approximate diameter of yarns may be found by extracting the square root of the yards per pound of the count. A deduction of 14% for crossbred worsted or 10% for Botany worsted will give very close results.

Example: What is the diameter of a yarn spun to 9s worsted (from crossbred fleece)?

9s worsted = 560 yards × 9 = 5,040 yards per pound.

$\sqrt{5,040} = 70 \cdot 99 - 14\%$ (9·93) = 61 ∴ 9s worsted = 1/61 in.

Conversion Table for Metric Measure

| in | mm | Diameter | |
		in	mm
1/64	0·39		
1/32	0·79	1/25	1·0
1/16	1·58	1/30	0·846
1/8	3·17	1/35	0·725
3/16	4·76	1/40	0·635
1/4	6·35	1/45	0·564
5/16	7·93	1/50	0·508
3/8	9·52	1/55	0·461
7/16	11·11	1/60	0·423
1/2	12·70	1/65	0·390
9/16	14·26	1/70	0·362
5/8	15·87	1/75	0·338
11/16	17·46	1/80	0·317
3/4	1·905	1/85	0·298
13/16	20·63	1/90	0·282
7/8	22·22	1/95	0·267
15/16	23·81	1/100	0·254
1	25·40		
12 (1 foot)	304·80		
24 (2 feet)	609·60		
36 (1 yard)	914·40		

Conversion Table (Metric/Imperial Measure)

Imperial oz	Metric g	Standard Imperial Units to Metric Values oz	Standard Imperial Units to Metric Values g	Standard Metric Units to approx. Imperial Values g	Standard Metric Units to approx. Imperial Values oz
$\frac{1}{4}$	7·09	$\frac{1}{4}$	7·09	1	1/28
$\frac{1}{2}$	14·17	$\frac{1}{2}$	14·17	2	1/14
$\frac{3}{4}$	21·26	1	28·35	5	1/5
1	28·35	2	56·70	10	1/3
$1\frac{1}{2}$	42·50	4 ($\frac{1}{4}$ lb)	113·40	20	2/3
$1\frac{3}{4}$	49·60	8 ($\frac{1}{2}$ lb)	226·80	50	$1\frac{3}{4}$
2	56·70	16 (1 lb)	453·59	100	$3\frac{1}{2}$
3	85·05			200	7
4 ($\frac{1}{4}$ lb)	113·40			250	$8\frac{3}{4}$
5	141·75			500 ($\frac{1}{2}$ kg)	$17\frac{1}{2}$
6	170·10			1000 (1 kg)	35
7	198·45				
8 ($\frac{1}{2}$ lb)	226·80				
9	255·15				
10	283·50				
11	311·85				
12 ($\frac{3}{4}$ lb)	340·19				
13	368·54				
14	396·89				
15	425·24				
16 (1 lb)	453·59				
17	481·94				
18	501·29				

Appendix IV
Yarn and Warp Sizing

C. Kretchmar, 1911 (in a translation from German) writes:

All that is necessary in sizing wool is to stiffen and protect it for weaving by means of glue or starch, and for this purpose the following recipes may serve as a guide:

No. 59   Recipe for Sizing Woollen Warps, on the Air-drying Machine: 11 lb (5 kg) of glue and 2¼ lb (1 kg) of glycerine are dissolved in 22 gallons (100 l) of water, the solution being used at about 104 °F (40 °C) (cold in the case of dyed warps), and dried slowly at medium temperature.

No. 60b   Recipe for Heavy Woollen Warps, on the Air-drying Machine: 22 gallons of water and 13¼ lb of maize starch are boiled for about half an hour. The size is used warm.

No. 61   Recipe for Fine Worsted Warps or Cheviots, on the Air-drying Machine: 22 gallons (100 l) of water are boiled for about fifteen minutes with 8¾ lb (4 kg) of maize starch and 6½ lb (3 kg) of cabinet-maker's glue, the latter having been previously soaked all night, and the starch and water stirred whilst being gradually raised to boiling. The size is applied at 140–160 °F (60–71 °C) and slow drying is recommended.

No. 62   Recipe for Fine Light Woollens, on the Air-drying Machine: 22 gallons (100 l) of water are boiled for twenty minutes with 13¼ lb (6 kg) of potato starch, 4½ lb (2 kg) of cabinet-maker's glue, 10 oz (284 g) of glycerine, 4 oz (113 g) of pure oil, and 4½ oz (128 g) of neutral Marseilles soap. Apply the size at 140–160 °F, and dry slowly.

Appendix V

Twist Direction as an Element in Fabric Design

In attempting to visualize the way that fibres in a yarn coil around the yarn axis, we have to remember that while the fibres on that part of the surface of the yarn which we can see may all incline, say, to the right (a 'Z' spun yarn), those on the underside will be sloping towards the left (Fig. 137).

It is a factor we should bear constantly in mind, for it can play a very important part in the appearance of the fabrics we are able to make from the yarns we produce.

This can be seen in Fig. 114 on page 141 where, in cross-section, a piece of woven fabric is illustrated which shows how the surfaces of the warp and weft threads are in contact with each other. The warp lies alternately over and under the weft, the top and bottom surface of the yarn being alternately in contact with the top or bottom surfaces of the weft threads.

In A on Fig. 138, where a 'Z' twisted warp is used with a 'Z' twisted weft, the yarns tend to merge into each other, because the fibres in those surfaces in contact all incline in the same direction, leading to enhanced felting and a dense fabric.

However, when the yarns used for warp are twisted contra to those used for weft, as in B Fig. 138 ('S' twisted warp and 'Z' twisted weft), the fibres lie across each other at the point of contact, and are thus less able to merge. The threadiness of the fabric is therefore enhanced. It is an area worthy of considerable experiment, some weaves—twills, for example, and fabrics chosen for shot effects—being particularly rewarding.

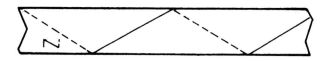

Fig. 137 Dotted lines represent fibres on the underside of the yarn which will incline in the opposite direction to those on the top.

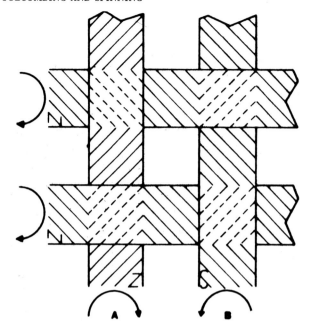

Fig. 138   Dotted lines show fibre direction on underside of top yarn. 'Z' spun warp will bed into 'Z' spun weft (A) but 'S' spun warp will stand clear of 'Z' spun weft because the fibres in contact will lie across each other (B). The arrows represent the spindle rotation in spinning.

Another interesting effect for the fabric designer is seen if two worsted spun yarns, one twisted 'S' and the other 'Z', are laid side by side. Because the fibres in the 'Z' twisted yarn all incline to the right (while those in the 'S' twisted yarn incline to the left), they will, under many differing lighting conditions, reflect varying qualities of light. This property can be used with great effect when warps are made of alternating groups of threads of, say, ten 'S', ten 'Z', etc. The fabric, either natural or coloured, will exhibit colour bars which vary in intensity and, of course, counter-change with the direction of the incident light.

Because all the yarns are dyed to the same shade and the colour variation is achieved by the twist direction and light deflection only, care must be taken in weaving to ensure that if any ends go down, they are pieced with yarns of the correct twist direction. The weaver may feel more confident if, prior to beaming, all yarn of one twist direction is tinted with a fugitive dye, which can be removed in finishing.

Appendix VI
Scouring of Yarn

As has already been shown on page 46, the scouring of twisted fibre may be more difficult and less effective than the scouring of fibre not under compression. However, yarn made from scoured fleece will only contain the spinning oil which has been used in processing, and this, we find, is readily removed if soapflakes are used as the scouring agent.

We use the same quantity and procedure as for fleece, except that normally only one steeping for about two hours is necessary. We tie the hank of yarn loosely every four inches or so to prevent tangling. Then, after steeping and wringing (or spinning) out most of the surplus rinsing water, we spread the yarn out evenly over a tensioning device to dry.

Index

1. Books, records, pictures circulate for 4 weeks (28 days)
2. Periodicals, 8mm films, cassettes and new books circulate for 2 weeks (14 days)
3. Only one renewal for 28 day items.
4. A fine will be charged for each overdue item at the rate of 2 cents per calendar day.
5. Video tapes circulate for one day.